Peter Carroll and Aynsley Kellow
The OECD: A Decade of Transformation

Peter Carroll and Aynsley Kellow

The OECD: A Decade of Transformation

—

2011–2021

DE GRUYTER

The opinions and arguments expressed herein are those of the authors and do not necessarily reflect the official views of the OECD or its member countries.

This document, as well as any data and map included herein, are without prejudice to the status of or sovereignty over any territory, to the delimitation of international frontiers and boundaries and to the name of any territory, city or area.

ISBN 978-3-11-073931-2
e-ISBN (PDF) 978-3-11-073583-3
e-ISBN (EPUB) 978-3-11-073588-8

Library of Congress Control Number: 2021940653

Bibliographic information published by the Deutsche Nationalbibliothek
The Deutsche Nationalbibliothek lists this publication in the Deutsche Nationalbibliografie; detailed bibliographic data are available on the internet at http://dnb.dnb.de.

© 2021 OECD
Published by Walter de Gruyter GmbH, Berlin/Boston
Cover image: OECD
Typesetting: Integra Software Services Pvt. Ltd.
Printing and binding: CPI books GmbH, Leck

www.degruyter.com

Leaders' Testimonials (December 2020)

This crisis highlights the role of the OECD, with its 60 years of experience in multi-lateral co-operation in formulating policies that promote transparency and governance, accommodating the evolving trends and the needs of the global economy as well as its positive contribution to the formulation of the required global path to tackle this unprecedented crisis, and the sought after solidarity in the efforts to alleviate the burden shouldered by all countries, regardless of their degree of development in addition to guiding such joint efforts to a win-win situation.

–**Abdel Fattah Al-Sisi**
President of Egypt

I want to warmly welcome the work of the OECD. Its commitment to values that are also ours: inclusion, equality, in particular gender equality, human dignity. All of which has been done in a remarkable way in recent years, thanks to the dynamism and determination of your dear Secretary-General Angel, who enabled the OECD to embody this ambitious multilateralism that we defend together.

–**Audrey Azoulay**
UNESCO Director General

With 60 years of experience, The OECD is the best example of how international co-operation can work to the benefit of its members, but also other actors, such as non-member countries or other international bodies.

–**Andrej Babiš**
Prime Minister of the Czech Republic

The OECD has deployed a remarkable depth of evidence-based analysis and promoted broad, multidisciplinary, multi-stakeholder policy approaches. My office has been proud to work with the OECD Secretariat on a range of vital human rights issues. It is the club of good practices.

–**Michelle Bachelet**
United Nations High Commissioner for Human Rights

Over the past six decades, the OECD has served as one of the internationally premier forums proposing solutions based on science and sharing exemplary policies with these member countries. Moreover, the OECD has spared no effort in collaborating with the United Nations. [. . .] The OECD should take the lead and serve as a Pathfinder

https://doi.org/10.1515/9783110735833-202

to advance this political momentum for Green New Deal and 2050 net zero targets into concrete actions.

–**Ban Ki-moon**
Former Secretary-General, United Nations

Since its foundation, the OECD, has proven to be a fundamental actor in the international context, providing not only an important forum and knowledge hub for data and analysis, but also for the exchange of experiences and best practice sharing. It has also been very relevant in advising on public policies and international standard settings in assisting countries in defining and implementing new policies and instruments for development. Particular importance has been given to middle income countries in their path towards development.

–**Alicia Bárcena**
Executive Secretary, Economic Commission for Latin America and the Caribbean

The speed with which the OECD has changed its tune to respond to the COVID crisis by putting all its knowledge at the service of economic recovery has impressed me. The OECD is firmly looking to the future. [. . .] you, the Secretary-General, dear Angel, have left an undeniable mark on the OECD. You have enhanced its status, its visibility, its relevance and I thank you from the bottom of my heart for having taken such good care of our Organisation.

–**Xavier Bettel**
Prime Minister of Luxembourg

The OECD can be proud. It has made people's lives better. You have been able to combine the rigorous analysis with an open mind to non-conventional thinking on most relevant fronts and new challenges. With your focus on people policy and your belief in public private partnerships and the key role of the private sector, it is no surprise that the G20 has turned to the OECD more than to any other organisation to be its de facto policy arm.

–**Ana Botín**
Executive Chairman, Santander Group

Over the years, the organisation has given an essential contribution as a catalyst for international consensus on economic issues and the global standard setter for the promotion of inclusive, sustainable growth policies, based on its accurate reports and analysis. Today its role is still to be able to contribute to a fair and inclusive economic development for the next generation.

–**Giuseppe Conte**
President of the Council of Ministers, Italy

I can also testify to the personal commitment of Angel Gurría, Secretary-General. We had the honour to host each of our events, including this year, our first virtual edition. A heartfelt thank you dear Angel for your precious support, contribution and key insights. You have always been a pillar in the Women's Forum Initiative including this year championing the initiative aiming to create the best conditions to promote women in leadership and governance worldwide.

–**Chiara Corazza**
Managing Director, Women's Forum

The OECD has never been more important than it is today for one essential reason. Never since World War II have our economies faced challenges of this magnitude. [. . .] The OECD has a unique role to play in these processes, with a forum for peer learning. Sharing for better learning.

–**António Costa**
Prime Minister of Portugal

The OECD has adapted to meet the challenges of its time. Under your leadership, Mr. Secretary-General, the Organisation has taken on the new challenges linked to the digitalisation of the economy, education, employment and the fight against inequalities. [. . .] May the OECD continue to be the international standard in the areas where it excels, while continuing to reinvent itself and adapt to the circumstances of the moment.

–**Alexander De Croo**
Prime Minister of Belgium

On behalf of the International Monetary Fund, I must sincerely commend the OECD for all the impressive work you have done over the last six decades to build better policies for better lives. We have been partners in many areas supporting inclusive and sustainable growth and improvements in living standards. We highly value your work on data and on evidence-based policy making and have benefited from your leadership on international standards, from taxation to anti-corruption.

–**Kristalina Georgieva**
IMF Managing-Director

The OECD plays an important role in the world's efforts to implement the 2030 Agenda for Sustainable Development, the Paris Agreement, the Addis Ababa Action Agenda and other frameworks for advancing human well being. It is a key norm setting body and a trusted source of data and analysis.

–**António Guterres**
Secretary-General of the United Nations

I would like to congratulate the OECD on its 60th anniversary and thank Angel Gurría and his colleagues for the wonderful, impactful work they are doing on development issues, particularly in the last decade. [. . .] The OECD has done so much, it still has a great deal to do. But its credibility as a development partner will continue to mean that it will enjoy the support and confidence of members and non-members alike for years to come.

–**Okonjo-Iweala**
Director General of the World Trade Organization

I would like to pay a special tribute to you, Secretary-General. Dear Ángel, I thank you for your engagement and friendship. You are leaving behind the organisation in an excellent shape, ready to confront the future challenges.

–**Janez Janša**
Prime Minister of Slovenia

I know, and I have often said that this Organisation is the number one think-tank on this planet, providing us with facts, numbers, figures, ideas, diagnosis, proposals that we need to build a better than what we have now planet. And as we know, this incredibly large COVID pandemic will leave us with a world in worse shape than the one before the crisis.

–**Pascal Lamy**
President of the Paris Peace Forum

At a time when science is being questioned and challenged, the OECD remains a beacon of trust and wisdom, as it has been for the past 60 years. [. . .] I would like to thank Secretary-General Gurría and recognise the achievements of the OECD under his leadership, not least during the current global health crisis.

–**Stefan Löfven**
Prime Minister of Sweden

It is quite clear to me that if the OECD did not exist today, we would have to invent it. [. . .] I would also like to congratulate Secretary-General Gurría, the secretariat, as well as all the member states and their OECD delegations in Paris on this special day and I wish you all good health.

–**Sanna Marin**
Prime Minister of Finland

The OECD draws on many strengths and values. Its member states share a commitment to democracy, human rights and the rule of law. And it is these shared strengths and values that underpin the well-earned trust we place in the OECD's authority and objectivity. Under Secretary General Gurría, the OECD has shown remarkable resilience and leadership, including in the context of the devastation caused by the COVID-19 pandemic.

–**Micheál Martin**
Taoiseach Ireland

The OECD has become a symbol of democratic values, a source of inspiration, and a driver of evidence-based policymaking.[. . .] A vision that will build on past achievements, but also on this very recent pandemic experience achieved under the leadership of Secretary-General Gurría. Dear Ángel, thank you for your excellent job and your friendship and support over the years.

–**Igor Matovič**
Prime Minister of the Slovak Republic

Submitting to international comparisons is sometimes unpleasant, but it often turns out to be extremely instructive. It is this, above all, that makes the OECD such an invaluable policy partner and so influential in international cooperation. [. . .] This is what it offers as a pioneer for international standards. And it provides momentum to this end with its knowledge platform which allows best practice comparisons. The importance of the OECD's work has been highlighted not least by the COVID-19 pandemic and its consequences.

–**Angela Merkel**
Chancellor, Federal Republic, Germany

Thanks to the work of the OECD, we are living in a fairer and more transparent world, and businesses could thrive on a level playing field. Korea has created its own success story as well by practicing universal values the OECD has been pursuing – democracy, human rights, market economy, and open economy.

–**Moon Jae-in**
President of the Republic of Korea

Today, after 60 years of existence, it is the OECD that can and in my opinion should play a special role in the development of foundations for this new economic order, implementing the organisation's slogan, "Better Policies for Better Lives".

–**Mateusz Morawiecki**
Prime Minister of Poland

For 60 years, the OECD has proven that better policies produce better lives. Because of your thoughtful and careful research and analysis, the health, the welfare, the education and the environment of untold millions of people is better. [. . .] The OECD is in a strong position to maximise the strength of a post COVID economic recovery. [. . .] I believe the methodology the OECD has pioneered and continues to develop will help us get to where we all want to be, but more importantly need to be, as like-minded countries.

–**Scott Morrison**
Prime Minister of Australia

Ángel, I want to congratulate you and commend you for the excellent work that you're doing and leading the OECD with wisdom, with patience and with a sense of mission. And the mission is to bring best practices to the economies of the world; we learn from each other, we help each other, and we support each other.

–**Benjamin Netanyahu**
Prime Minister of Israel

A particularly memorable event for me was the visit by the Secretary-General Gurría and OECD staff to Japan in April 2011, soon after the Great East Japan Earthquake. At that time most of the scheduled visits from foreign countries had been cancelled, but the OECD team visited us as per schedule. Secretary-General Gurría gave us the message that "we are assured that the bad effect of the earthquake to the Japanese economy won't last long, and we would recover very soon", which encouraged us a lot. I truly appreciate the OECD's support to our effort of recovery under the strong leadership of Secretary-General Gurría.

–**Toshihiro Nikai**
Secretary-General of the Japanese Liberal Democratic Party and President,
Friends of the OECD in Japan

The OECD has been a force for good, joining the best causes of humanity. It has done so during the last 60 years but this has magnified under the visionary and powerful leadership of Secretary-General Angel Gurría, who I had the pleasure to work with as his chief of staff and Sherpa. [. . .] He has led with his evidence, with his standards, and more than anything, with his passion. From supporting the French presidency of

COP 21, to fighting monopolies and corruption, to promoting good governance in Mexican telecoms, and revamping the anti-bribery laws in Greece. [. . .] These achievements build on the fantastic legacy of Secretary-General Gurría. The OECD has made history and we're so proud of it. It needs to continue delivering. Long live the OECD.

–**Gabriela Ramos**
Assistant Director-General, UNESCO

I'm delighted to say that today, 60 years later, the OECD is more vital and more relevant than ever. [. . .] The organisation has always been a driving force behind the multilateral system that fosters global cooperation. A robust organisation that helps to build and maintain a rules-based international system. So, 60 years after the signing of the convention, we can conclude, not only that the OECD has achieved a lot over the decades, but also there's a lot more work that lies ahead.

–**Mark Rutte**
Prime Minister of the Netherlands

The OECD has become an ever more important and influential actor and partner on the multilateral scene, supporting and complementing the actions of the United Nations system, as well as international financial and economic institutions on a wide range of issues. [. . .] I think that there has been no time over the past 60 years when our two organisations have worked so well together. And I want to thank Secretary-General Gurría for making this happen.

–**Guy Ryder**
Director-General, International Labour Organization

It has been the prime intergovernmental forum for sharing and spreading best practices in public policymaking in fields such as education, fiscal affairs, public governance, digital economy, environment, responsible business conduct, public integrity, regulatory policies, amongst others, and the one I know best first hand, science and technology policies.

–**Francisco Sagasti**
President of the Republic of Peru

The OECD has helped us to rethink and improve the foundations of our economic and social system and for this we are grateful to the OECD. [. . .] It is up to the OECD to identify the best practices, the useful practices, the possible ones, that can enable us to face the challenge of change and the fight against inequality together. [. . .]

Which is why the OECD must reaffirm its role in the fight for fiscal justice. [. . .] and the help of the OECD is fundamental, essential to put together this chain of values.

–David Sassoli
President of the European Parliament

For 60 years, the OECD has been unique in the multilateral family. OECD has facilitated political decisions based on science, through its data collection, and research. The organisation has also been an important standard setter for international development. We have learnt from each other at the OECD and this will continue to be important. The OECD has been and continues to be a central part of our coordinated efforts.

–Erna Solberg
Prime Minister of Norway

Thanks to your impetus Secretary-General, the OECD has become an essential organisation in world economic governance. As fiscal and monetary policies reach their limits, structural policies gain in importance. The OECD therefore has a central role to play in helping Member States design policies capable of meeting the challenges of our time.

–Simonetta Sommaruga
President of the Swiss Federation

The OECD has significantly contributed to strengthening the multilateral free trade system and to sustainable economic growth through evidence-based analysis and quality standard setting. Japan highly appreciates such efforts by the OECD. [. . .] At this critical juncture, the role of OECD to gather our wisdom from around the world and to coordinate policies has never been more important.

–Yoshihide Suga
Prime Minister of Japan

For 60 years, the Organisation for Economic Co-operation and Development has worked diligently to build better policies for better lives. [. . .] Canada believes that the OECD can be a driving force in strengthening multilateralism, supporting a strong recovery and building a more resilient world.

–Justin Trudeau
Prime Minister of Canada

I congratulate the OECD on its 60th anniversary. Under the leadership of José Angel Gurría, Indonesia and the OECD have forged a stronger partnership. This is reflected through the establishment of the OECD Jakarta Office and the continuation of the Indonesia-OECD Framework of Co-operation Agreement. Going forward, sound policies and international collaboration are needed to ensure a global recovery in the post COVID pandemic context. I hope a stronger OECD presence in Southeast Asia will also contribute to regional economic growth and prosperity. As a key OECD partner and an incoming G20 President 2022, Indonesia looks forward to further enhancing mutual co-operation with the OECD.

–**Joko Widodo**
President of the Republic of Indonesia

Acknowledgements

This book has been written under conditions not typical for academic work, with the brief being to prepare a history of the achievements of the OECD from 2011 to 2021. We had previously written a volume that coincided with the first 50 years of the OECD, demonstrating its adaptability in the face of changing circumstances. This volume shows how that adaptability reached new heights, leading to a substantial transformation of the OECD, despite the challenges of the global financial crisis and then the COVID-19 pandemic.

The relatively short period available for researching and writing this book made the assistance we received from many people all the more important, especially those who kindly participated in almost 70 Zoom interviews – including Secretary-General Angel Gurría,[*] other members of the Secretariat past and present, and several Ambassadors to the OECD. These were conducted on a confidential not-for-attribution basis and they added much detail to the story told in documents.

For access to a wealth of documentary material we thank Juan Yermo, the OECD Chief of Staff, but especially Kostas Panagiotopoulos from the Office of the Secretary-General. It is difficult to imagine that we could have written the book without assistance from Kostas, who managed to find countless documents we requested, clarify many uncertain facts, and – importantly – arrange the Zoom interviews from December 2020 through to April 2021, always faultlessly despite the challenges of differing time zones between Hobart and Paris and other locations. We would like to thank Patrick Love for copyediting the manuscript.

Finally, we thank our families for their forbearance during a summer that was rather fully occupied by things OECD.

Peter Carroll and Aynsley Kellow
Hobart, Tasmania, Australia
April 2021

---

[*] The writing of this book was completed in May 2021 while Angel Gurría was in office as the Secretary General of the OECD. On 1 June 2021, Mathias Cormann was appointed to this position for a five-year term.

https://doi.org/10.1515/9783110735833-203

Contents

1 Introduction

The Organisation for Economic Co-operation and Development (OECD) occupies a unique place in the global architecture of international economic governance. Its origins lie in the Marshall Plan, an American initiative to help rebuild European economies after the end of the Second World War in the face of a growing Soviet threat. A new organisation, the Organisation for European Economic Co-operation (OEEC), was established in 1948 to administer the Marshall Plan. The OEEC also helped to build a co-operative spirit among Western European economies as they searched for policy solutions to the challenges they faced.

The OECD was formed from the OEEC through its Members' desire to carry forward its work on a wider stage. A founding convention for the OECD was negotiated and concluded in Paris on 14 December 1960 among the existing 18 OEEC members plus the US and Canada, the latter two becoming full Members of the new organisation. The OECD came formally into being on 30 September 1961, and its Members all had, and still have, a commitment to the core goal of developing policies and agreements that foster sustainable economic growth. The goal of this growth is to improve the lives of OECD Members' citizens, and the citizens of non-member countries, with a commitment to liberal democratic norms. As a result, there is considerable 'like-mindedness' among Members, as well as considerable sharing of policy learning. This often leads to policy transfer, achieved through such processes as subjecting Members' policies to the discipline of 'peer review' by other Members, as well as policy research by the Secretariat, with a strong emphasis on developing evidence-based, comparative policy options.

This core, policy-focused goal has not changed in the 60 years of the OECD's existence, for two basic reasons. The first is that the overall goal and associated aims in its founding Convention are sufficiently broad to permit OECD Members to undertake almost any activity they wish in relation to economic growth, trade and stability. This, in turn, provides Members with a relatively high degree of flexibility when faced with changing conditions, such as those so dramatically posed by the global financial crisis, COVID-19, and the recent rise in multilateral tensions. The second reason is the relative homogeneity of Members' fundamental political and economic values. Which is not to assert that they have no differences, for they have many, as is evident in their debates, discussions and arguments on a vast range of topics. The differences, however, are not so great as to conflict in any fundamental way with the OECD's overall goal. The increasingly rigorous process of accession to the Organisation enables Members to exclude those whose perspectives are too different.

This inherent, organisational adaptability has been brought to the fore in the decade from 2011 to 2021, a period of widespread transformation of the OECD, examined at greater length in the following chapters. During these 10 years:

https://doi.org/10.1515/9783110735833-001

- The membership of the OECD has increased from 34 to 37 (and soon, with Costa Rica's membership, to 38).
- The number of staff rose sharply, up from 2,500 to approximately 3,700, driven largely by voluntary contributions.
- The governance of the Organisation was reformed.
- Global relations were substantially expanded, with an emphasis on disseminating OECD standards throughout the world and, in particular, much wider access to participation in the OECD's work by non-members.
- The finances of the Organisation were reformed, prioritising improved efficiency.
- Human resources policies were reformed and various management initiatives were launched.
- A wide range of policies, initiatives, agreements and standards were either introduced or substantially modified, making the OECD the hub of an extensive, global policy network and increasing its impact and relevance.

While the number of books and articles about the OECD published in the last decade has grown rapidly, in line with its growing importance in global economic governance, most have focused on one or more periods before 2011–2021. Yet, this latter period has been one in which the OECD experienced the most rapid series of changes since its founding in 1961, amounting to a veritable transformation of the Organisation. It was also a period that saw the last two of three terms in office of Secretary-General Angel Gurría, who has occupied that position for 15 years, matched only by Emile van Lennep's tenure from 1969 to 1984. Hence, the aim of this book is to provide a description of the life of the OECD, covering the period from 2011, the year of its 50th anniversary, to 2021, its 60th anniversary.

This is a relatively short book, so several of the changes experienced at the OECD are not covered, not because they are unimportant, but simply because of a lack of space. Similarly, most of the major changes that are covered in the book are not covered in any great depth, leaving opportunities for other scholars to provide the depth of analysis they deserve. Moreover, as the book is intended for a general audience, we have not provided what would have been a very extensive set of references to support our description and analysis. Nevertheless, most of the documents and developments noted in the text can be found on the OECD's website.

In the many interviews conducted by the authors we apologised, in advance, to the interviewees for what we knew would be the omission of many interesting facts and opinions that they would provide, and we take this opportunity to once again apologise. Even where their views and anecdotes are not included, they provided a 'flavour' to this work for which we are very grateful.

The book consists of 13 chapters. Chapters 2 and 3 are intended, primarily, for those readers unfamiliar with the OECD and focus on how the Organisation is governed and its remarkable history.

Chapter 4, on leadership, is a topic that has been rather neglected in previous studies of the OECD. It concentrates on the leadership of Secretary-General Gurría, who has led the Organisation through a period of great change, marked by the impact of the global financial crisis (GFC) and COVID-19.

Chapter 5 covers the rapidly growing, and increasingly important, global work of the OECD, especially the development and implementation of a new global relations strategy, the Organisation's enlargement and, particularly in its relations with the G7/G8 and the G20, its success in positioning itself as a hub of a global policy network.

Chapter 6, 'Going National', describes the increased efforts by the Organisation to provide even more relevant policy work for its Members, with a sharpened focus on tailoring policy solutions to national contexts and providing advice on their implementation.

Chapter 7 examines the 'Green Growth' initiative that helped fully establish the environmental credentials of the OECD, with its work on the increasingly important issues of the economics of climate change and biodiversity.

Chapter 8 illustrates how the Organisation has led the world by focusing on well-being and inclusive growth, rather than primarily on GDP, developing statistical techniques to measure them.

Chapter 9 looks at innovation and the digital economy, areas of work that have both grown and become more interconnected at the OECD over the last decade, and are likely to continue to grow in the years ahead. It is also work that has taken care to examine the social dimensions of both innovation and the digital economy, in line with the OECD's work on inclusion.

Chapter 10 looks at the long and very successful experience of the OECD with work on taxation and tax administration, leading to its present position as the preeminent international agency in the field, a position that has helped enhance the OECD's global reputation.

Chapter 11 looks at New Approaches to Economic Challenges (NAEC), Strategic Foresight and Smart Data. NAEC is a unit driving the ongoing attempt to develop new, more sophisticated understandings of socio-economic systems that could better support and, where appropriate, modify and overturn traditional assumptions and the OECD's economic and social policy analysis and recommendations built upon them. Strategic Foresight, like NAEC, based in the Office of the Secretary-General, provides assistance in using ideas and scenarios about the future that can be used to better anticipate change and policies for dealing with that change. The Smart Data project aims to help meet policy needs with innovative data, technical, organisational, legal and human capabilities, working closely with OECD Member countries and the broader data ecosystem.

Chapter 12 examines OECD work on health, which became a central focus in the last two decades, and then on COVID-19, the subject of rapidly expanding work as regards its impact since its onset in 2020. This will expand as the world recovers from the pandemic.

Chapter 13 is a short conclusion, summarising what the authors regard as the major changes at the OECD in the last decade, a period of transformation.

2 How the Organisation Works

This chapter outlines the major organisational units and decision processes that characterise the OECD for those readers unfamiliar with the Organisation. It should be noted that, over time, modifications to these units and processes have and will continue to take place. The budgetary system, for example, was substantially modified in 1995–2003, more firmly locating it as a key component of the Organisation's strategic management process.

The OECD Council

The OECD Council is composed of representatives of all OECD Members as well as of the European Union. It is the governing body of the Organisation and is chaired by the OECD Secretary-General. The Council consists of Permanent Representatives, meeting usually on a monthly basis, consisting mostly of senior public servants from Member countries with the rank of Ambassador, who lead their Delegations. Once a year, the Council meets at Ministerial level with Ministers drawn from all Members, a meeting known as the Ministerial Council (MCM). The MCM meets to discuss the Strategic Orientations of the Secretary-General, and to endorse a set of priorities for continuing and future OECD work. The chair of the MCM is drawn annually from one of its Members.

The Council has four major roles. The first is a continuing process whereby it assesses the political and whole of government implications of the issues placed before it by the Secretary-General, and makes a range of substantive decisions. The second is providing strategic direction for the OECD by identifying and agreeing strategic priorities to be taken into consideration in the development of the work plans and budgets prepared for its later approval. The third role of the Council is resource allocation, centred in OECD's budgetary process. The fourth role is evaluating the Organisation's overall performance, including the evaluation of Committees.

The Council is supported in its work by three Standing Committees, the Executive, Budget, and the External Relations Committees, which filter and transmit to the Council reports, proposals or documents with comments and suggested amendments when needed, leaving the Council free to focus on major concerns. In addition, the Council is assisted by a number of special bodies, including the following:
– Audit Committee
– Evaluation Committee
– Pension Budget and Reserve Fund Management Board

The Council is also supported once a year by the organisation of the Global Strategy Group. This Group, with high-level participation from capitals, is the current format of a body whose origins go back to the 1970s. It has met since 2012 to discuss major issues

https://doi.org/10.1515/9783110735833-002

and to assess their potential impact on the design and implementation of policy reforms. It also helps shape the MCM agenda and setting the Organisation's priorities.

Since the creation of the OECD in 1961, around 480 substantive legal instruments have been developed. These include OECD Acts (i.e. the Decisions and Recommendations adopted by the OECD Council in accordance with the OECD Convention) and other legal instruments developed within the OECD framework (e.g. Declarations, international agreements). OECD Decisions are legally binding on all adherents and entail the same kind of legal obligations as international treaties. Adherents are obliged to implement Decisions and must take the necessary measures for their implementation. OECD Recommendations are not legally binding – they represent a political commitment to the principles and policy approaches they contain and entail an expectation that adherents will do their best to implement them.

Council also adopts Resolutions, which are internal decisions concerning the continuation of the work of the Organisation. These usually relate to the renewal of the mandate of a substantive Committee or to procedural, budgetary or administrative issues.

In practice it is rare for Council to reject any proposal for a Decision, Resolution, or Recommendation as proposals likely to be highly sensitive, contentious or divisive are dealt with informally or in earlier discussions as part of the consensus-building process in one of the standing or substantive Committees, with all parties mindful of the requirement for consensus.

The Secretary-General

The Secretary-General is appointed by the Council for a period of five years to assist it in all 'appropriate ways', and contributes to the strategic direction of the Organisation and ensures its institutional coherence. The Secretary-General has the right to submit proposals to Council and any other body of the Organisation. The position is responsible for implementing Council decisions, including the Programme of Work and Budget (PWB), and for appointing staff, though subject to Council approval of organisational plans and staff regulations. Article 11(2) of the OECD's Convention makes it clear that the Secretariat, the OECD's staff, are to be independent, by specifying that staff:

> . . . shall neither seek nor receive instructions from any of the Members or from any Government or authority external to the Organisation

They are independent of the individual Members and external authorities, but they report to the Secretary-General who, in turn, is responsible to the Council. Most OECD publications are also released under the Secretary-General's authority (with the exception of the Economic and Development Review Committee -EDRC – Country Surveys), providing for greater independence in analysis and recommendations while still ensuring Members' review via the Committees.

During the period covered by this book, the Secretary-General was Angel Gurría, first appointed in June 2006 and who completed his third five-year term in office in May 2021. In his 15 years as Secretary-General, he has provided strong, continuing leadership that has established and maintained the OECD as a central actor in global economic governance, working with the G20, G7, IMF, WTO, World Bank, ASEAN, the EU and the Asia-Pacific Economic Cooperation (APEC).

The Cabinet of the Secretary-General consists of the senior management team of currently three Deputy Secretaries-General, each with a range of specific responsibilities, plus a Chief of Staff, currently Mr Juan Yermo, who leads the Office of the Secretary-General. The team is supported by the Deputy Chief of Staff and a varying number of specialist advisors, together with the Heads of the Strategic Foresight Unit, the New Approaches to Economic Challenges (NAEC) Unit, the Speech Writing and Intelligence Unit, the Global Governance and Sherpa Unit, and a Protocol and Resource Management Unit.

Also at the centre of the Organisation are the General Secretariat, the Executive Secretariat and the Public Affairs and Communications Directorate. The General Secretariat consists of the Council and Executive Committee Secretariat, the Directorate for Legal Affairs, the Global Relations Secretariat and Internal Audit. The Council and Executive Committee Secretariat supports the Secretary-General in maintaining strong relations with Member countries and their Delegations in the Council, ensuring the implementation of mandates related to the Organisation's work and advancing its strategic objectives. It contributes to effective governance by providing key operational support to the Council and its Executive Committee and related meetings, and advice and assistance on institutional and procedural issues to Delegations and the Secretariat. It also liaises with the Directorate for Legal Affairs and other teams supporting the OECD's Standing Committees to ensure appropriate coordination and support efficient decision-making. The Director of the Council and Executive Committee Secretariat, in particular, maintains close relations with, and supports, the Permanent Delegations in their role in OECD governance, and also supports the Secretary-General in his role as Chair of Council.

The Directorate for Legal Affairs provides advice and information on the legal, institutional and procedural aspects of the OECD's activities, particularly the negotiation, interpretation and application of its legal instruments; ensures that the privileges, immunities, and legal status of the Organisation are respected, and handles any litigation involving the Organisation. It also assists in the formulation, amendment and implementation of internal rules and regulations, including the Rules of Procedure, Staff Regulations and Financial Regulations, and provides legal advice relating to procurement and some financial contributions. Increasingly, it advises on relations with non-members and other international organisations, and serves as the coordinator of the process for accession to the Organisation. The latter is a time-consuming task that usually requires the recruitment of additional staff, with the Directorate acting as an interpreter of legal instruments for both OECD and candidate countries.

The Global Relations Secretariat is responsible for managing the OECD's relations with Brazil, China, India, Indonesia and South Africa, as well as with the regions of Southeast Asia, Latin America and the Caribbean, South East Europe, Central Asia and the MENA region. It supports the Secretary-General's objectives for a regionally inclusive and globally relevant organisation and, in line with the growing importance of the OECD's Global Relations Strategy has grown considerably in size over the last decade, centralising a number of staff previously scattered across a number of Directorates.

Internal Audit, established in 2003, is headed by a Director and reports to the Secretary-General. It provides the Secretary-General with an independent and objective assurance and advisory activity, undertaking systematic evaluation aimed at improving the effectiveness of governance, risk management, and control processes. It is supervised by Council's Audit Committee, which monitors the independence and effectiveness of the internal and external audit functions, and reviews the financial situation of the Organisation. The Committee consists of nine members designated by Council, six nominated from permanent Delegations of Member countries, including ex officio the Chair of the Budget Committee, and three expert members proposed by the Supreme Audit Institutions of Member countries.

The Executive Directorate is responsible for managing and coordinating the OECD's corporate services, including financial and human resource management, information technology, internal communications, conference management, security, translation and interpretation, building infrastructure and logistics. The Public Affairs and Communications Directorate is responsible for developing and implementing the OECD's public affairs, communications and engagement strategies, such as 'Better Policies for Better Lives', and engagement with all non-government stakeholders.

The Role of the Delegations

All OECD Members maintain a permanent Delegation in Paris and they have four key tasks. First is to represent their countries in the OECD's governing bodies. In addition, most permanent Delegation staff occasionally represent their countries on a small number of Committees and their subsidiary bodies. Second, they liaise closely with their relevant national departments and agencies on all matters likely to be of interest, and share documents, reports and other relevant information. Third, they liaise closely with the Secretariat staff that undertake the relevant Committee work programmes, gaining a detailed knowledge of the Organisation. Fourth, while the major, substantive Committees are nearly always attended by delegates sent directly from national capitals, the Delegations provide varying degrees of support for capital city delegates, occasionally accompanying them to meetings.

The Heads of Delegations are the Ambassadors that constitute the Council, with overall responsibility for representing their countries' interests at the OECD. As well as sitting as members of Council they often have particular responsibilities as chairs, vice-chairs or members of Council's Standing Committees and Special Bodies. In addition, they gather informally as members of one or more of the broad 'factional', groupings of members, notably the EU, Nordic, APEC and G7 groups, to identify, develop and pursue common interests across a wide range of issues, including key policy, structural and process issues.

The OECD Substantive Committees and their Subsidiary Bodies

The Committees, and their three hundred plus subsidiary bodies (the number varies over time), are the Organisation's beating heart, for, as an OECD working party noted:

> Through its Committee structure the OECD's substantive policy agenda and outputs respond directly to the needs of, and are closely monitored by, senior policy officials from capitals in a way that may be unique among international organisations. It is these Committees that produce the outputs of the OECD, the policy advice, guidelines, principles ('soft law') and best practices. The working methods of the Committees are one of the institution's hallmarks, the source of its added value and the support it enjoys in capitals.[1]

The 36 substantive Committees are key actors that play a major role in determining the complex and dynamic agenda of the OECD. Indeed, it is more accurate to speak of the agendas of the OECD, rather than one agenda, with each substantive Committee developing and pursuing its own programme of work, subject to the agreement of Council, which sets the overall agenda. The key substantive Committees commonly delegate a range of responsibilities to various sub-Committees and groups.

The membership of the Committees varies depending on the role of the Committee in question. Many include several non-Members, especially countries targeted for enhanced engagement (Key Partners), Brazil, China, India, Indonesia and South Africa and a range of observers, for example, the WHO, IMF and World Bank. However, most of the delegates consist of representatives from Member governments, drawn either from the permanent Delegations or from domestic departments or agencies ('capital-based delegates'). Some national departments, notably Finance or Treasury departments, assign their high performing staff to their Paris Delegation for one or two years in order to gain experience in discussions and negotiations at the international level.

In general, the Committees meet only once or twice a year, for two or three days per session, but Members correspond frequently between the meetings in Paris. The Part I resources allocated in support of work overseen by the policy Committees vary

---

1 OECD (2006), *Resolution of the Council on a New Governance Structure for the Organisation,* Adopted by the Council at its 1135th session on 11 May 2006 [C/M(2006)9/PROV, Item 124], https://www.oecd.org/officialdocuments/publicdisplaydocumentpdf/?cote=C(2006)78/FINAL&docLanguage=En

substantially. The largest seven Committees and their subsidiaries are allocated over 50% of the Part I resources (excluding corporate areas). The differences in resource allocation are largely determined by differences in the extent and type of work undertaken for the Committees by the Secretariat. Those responsible for large-scale data gathering and analysis activities, especially when combined with major peer review activities, typically require and gain the largest share of resources, such as the Economic and Development Review Committee (EDRC), Economic Policy, Environment, Trade and Agriculture.

Most Committees and their subsidiary bodies are led by a small 'bureau' of Committee members. A secretary drawn from the staff of an OECD Directorate supports their work, which consists of between-meeting, networked activities and the meeting itself. The bulk of the substantive work is undertaken by the OECD Secretariat supported by the bureau, usually providing advice in reply to questions raised by its support staff in the relevant Directorate, and commenting upon drafts or part drafts of forthcoming reports on work authorised by the Committee. The Committees report to Council and, via the Members, to their respective national agencies.

While agendas vary, typically they include: progress reports on projects prepared by OECD staff; draft final project documents for consideration, including draft Recommendations; initial proposals for new or modified projects; notes and related documentation from the Secretary-General on OECD-wide matters; occasional papers prepared by experts external to the Committee, sometimes for presentation at the next meeting. Most of the documents for the meetings are prepared by OECD staff.

An important part of the work is the OECD's well-regarded system of peer review, which consists of an examination of one Member's performance or practices in a particular policy area by other Members. These provide both a means of subjecting the policies of Member countries to peer critical scrutiny – a 'quality assurance' check – and a means of identifying and sharing best practice among the membership (and beyond). One example is the economic surveys of Members that are conducted every 18 months by the EDRC, assessing the performance of that country in relation to a broad set of guidelines. Non-members, including China, India and Brazil, now also take part in the surveys. Another example is the peer review of implementation of OECD standards, such as the Working Group on Bribery's monitoring of the Anti-Bribery Convention, or the Global Forum on Tax Transparency and Exchange of Information reviews of the exchange of information standards.

The OECD decision-making is largely on the basis of mutual agreement, that is, by consensus, as specified in the Convention, which makes no distinction between more important or less important decisions. However, Council has adopted a limited variety of qualified majority voting (QMV) procedures for specified matters in Council and, when delegated, in the Standing Committees. Under QMV, decisions supported by at least 60% of Members are adopted, unless opposed by three or more Members representing at least 25% of the Part I scale of contributions of the Budget. In practice, the QMV procedure is rarely, if ever, utilised.

In all significant issues any decision can be blocked by even one dissenting vote. However, in practice, the consensus principle only presents difficulties where there are major and persisting differences between Members. This is because all Members appreciate that unreasonable, frequent refusals to reach agreement by a Member would lead to a similar response from other Members, a perception that acts as an effective constraint.

On relatively minor issues consultation is largely confined to the Committee. Larger, more complex issues require more extensive consultation by Committee and bureau members, possibly including discussion in the regular meetings of Heads of Delegation and, for issues such as the accession of new Members, discussions between foreign affairs departments outside of the OECD and other interested parties. Consultation can and does take place at any time and can be frequent and intense.

The Programme of Work and Budget (PWB)

The OECD's Budget is funded by Member contributions on a biennial basis, known as the Programme of Work and Budget (PWB). The results-based PWB is developed within the context of the OECD's Strategic Management Framework, based on six Strategic Objectives derived from the OECD Convention. The Strategic Objectives cascade down to Output Groups and, at a lower level, to Output Areas. The Strategic Management Framework provides the basis for Council decisions on resource allocation and for committee planning, budgeting and reporting.

The OECD's Budget is divided into two parts. The Part I Budget is funded by contributions from all OECD Members, based on a formula which takes account of the size of each Member's economy. For 2020, the Part II budget was MEUR 202.5. Part II Programmes are of common interest to a limited number of Members, or relate to sectors of activity not covered by Part I. Part II Programmes are funded according to scales of contributions or other financing arrangements agreed to by the participating Member countries. For 2020, the Part II Budget represented MEUR 109. There are 24 Part II Programmes that are fully integrated into the OECD's Strategic Management Framework, though they vary considerably in terms of membership, financing arrangements and governance. Examples of such programmes include International Energy Agency (IEA), International Transport Forum (ITF), and the Nuclear Energy Agency (NEA). Voluntary contributions, which are increasingly important, complement funding for both the Part I and Part II Budget and come from a variety of sources, notably Members and, in particular, the EU.

In summary, the PWB process begins with each Committee considering its budget proposal for the next two years, the actual draft(s) being drawn up by the more senior officials in the Directorate, based on the broader, strategic orientations developed by the Secretary-General and the Ambassadors' Informal Convergence Paper. Each draft is the result of a complex process of communication, negotiation, bargaining and co-ordination between internal and external stakeholders. The officials draw up the successive drafts for final approval by the relevant Committee. The PWB is then presented to the OECD's Budget Committee for consideration as part of the Secretary-General's consolidated, draft PWB for the Organisation as a whole. The Budget Committee then submits it to the Council for approval, with a list of its recommendations for the Council's consideration. In practice, the Council does not usually involve itself with the detail of the PWB, as the Budget Committee acts as a filter, leaving only the unresolved issues for Council to determine. As with all organisations the PWB process is an intensely political one, embracing a wide variety of national and organisational interests.

The Staff of the OECD

The current number of staff is approximately 3700, most undertaking work for substantive bodies. About 56% of staff are directly involved in policy analysis, producing key outputs and data e.g., economists, policy analysts and statisticians. These roles require an advanced degree, with three to 10 years' relevant professional experience. Executive leadership represents 5% of total staff; it includes the roles of Director, Deputy Director and Heads of Division, who design, lead and steer the OECD work programme and its staff to achieve strategic objectives. The senior staff are expected to have considerable senior-level experience in an international context, the ability to lead discussions in substantive bodies, 'very wide' experience in a national and international policy context in a relevant field, and 'political judgement'. 39% of staff manage the OECD's corporate activities (communication, human resources, information technology, buildings, conference facilities and security, language services and general management and administration).

While OECD staff and their work are usually highly regarded by Members, three factors bring about continuing concerns over staff capacity and objectivity in a number of areas: the sharp budget cutbacks that commenced in the 1990s; the continued, very tight budgetary constraints that followed that reduction, combined with increasing workload, leading to increased pressures on remaining staff; and the increasing significance of voluntary contributions (VCs), with their focus often on short-term projects staffed partly by staff on temporary contracts, officials seconded from national administrations or/and by external consultants. The increasing number of VC funded projects, whose progress is dependent upon maintaining funding support from a limited number of Members, led to the establishment of more fully-coordinated Voluntary Contribution Management Control Framework in 2017 with a Focal Point in the Office of the Secretary-General (OSG) updated in 2019. This helps ensure that VCs are fully integrated into the PWB. The Budget Committee receives regular reports on VCs and the Chief of Staff in the OSG works with a VC extended coordination group consisting of representatives of all directorates.

Recent Reforms: Governance, Finance and Human Resources

As indicated in the Introduction, modifications to the organisation and decision processes of the OECD are by no means uncommon, although they became more frequent in the period from the late 1990s to 2019. This followed slow progress on attempted reforms to operations, with Secretary-General Don Johnston preparing a 2001 paper noting his frustrations with the operation of the Organisation. Later the same year he produced a further paper, 'Committee Reform: A Big Bang Approach', outlining radical proposals to address his concerns. He was particularly concerned about his perceived inability to manage the Directorates, seeing several as 'silos' operating as fiefdoms, supported by their corresponding Committees and relevant national agencies. This limited the capacity of the Secretary-General, the Council and Budget Committee to prioritise OECD work to meet changing needs, such as by undertaking 'horizontal work' across a range of substantive bodies, which were generally given low priority.

However, in the following period, under Secretary-General Angel Gurría, a number of significant reforms, all built on earlier developments, were undertaken. One reform was related to the governance of the Organisation, with the objective to ensure that it keeps up with the evolution of the Members' needs and the Organisation's effectiveness in their delivery. Since the mid-2000s, four major governance review exercises have been undertaken, in 2006, 2010, 2014 and 2019 during which Members have discussed all issues they thought of relevance to the future governance of the OECD.

The 2006 exercise was the first comprehensive review of the governance of the Organisation since its creation, and notably established three decision-making methods and categories (fundamental cases, special cases coming under Qualified Majority Vote – QMV, and normal cases); institutionalised three Standing Committees (Executive Committee, Budget Committee and External Relations Committee) with specific mandates, and established the delegation of some decisions to these Standing Committees.

The 2010 Council Working Group on Governance review notably focused on the roles and mandates of the Standing Committees and Advisory Groups and the new QMV. In the 2014 exercise, the importance of consensus in decision making as a defining principle for the Organisation was underlined and some improvements identified in its decision-making process, with clarifications brought to the categories of cases and of procedures in the implementation of QMV, which resulted in a Revised Resolution on Governance.

The 2014 exercise resulted in 52 recommendations on the OECD's decision-making, working methods, covering priority setting, global relations, working methods of OECD Committees, horizontal projects and other issues, whose implementation was assessed in 2019 and is currently the subject of a follow-up exercise. As is normally the case, the governance reviews were serviced by the Secretariat, which in 2019 was given the task of assessing the implementation of the recommendations made in 2014. This assessment found that the QMV changes had, in practice, been of limited use, although they seem to have acted as an incentive for member to reach consensus; that priority setting had been strengthened, although it was time-consuming; that global relations had been strengthened; and the working methods of Committees had been improved, with the OLIS information system being replaced with the ONE Members & Partners system. The review was discussed by Council.

Another reform was the Value for Money (V4M) Project undertaken in 2013–2014, to assess the OECD's cost structure and the way outputs were produced, and which now takes place on a biennial basis.

A further reform was a linked series of human resource management reforms. They commenced after a comprehensive review of human resource management policies in 2005–2006 leading to an approved plan to implement the approved reforms. This began with the recruitment process, emphasizing two aspects: a merit-based recruitment system, achieving a better mix of nationalities enabling a greater variety of different ideas and perspectives; and an improved gender balance at all levels (there was a marked preponderance of men at senior levels). In addition, it was planned to move to a results-based staffing system with simplified employment categories, to revise the existing contract policy, improve the use of loans, exchanges and secondments, and provide flexible end-of-career provisions. The reforms commenced in 2008, but did not include the Secretary-General's authority to directly appoint the position's closest personal collaborators, the Chief of Staff, Deputy Chief of Staff, Chief Economist and the Executive Director.

In 2010 a comprehensive Employment Framework was approved by Council, which aligned HRM policies with the decentralisation of the financial resources to Part I Directorates and Services that was being undertaken. This followed the 2008 review of the staff performance evaluation system that aligned PWB outputs and the individual objectives of staff members. In 2014, the performance management system was modified to ensure managers improved their use of the system and better address poor performance. A new employment package was proposed in 2019, aimed at ensuring the continued attractiveness of the OECD as an employer and combat an increasing level of insecurity. Understanding the motivational drivers of current and future employees, and responding to them in a cost-efficient manner, is fundamental for any organisation. Responding to employee needs allows the OECD to deliver better on its mission, make the best use of resources and respond to its Members' needs.

Conclusion

In the decade 2011 to 2021, the OECD introduced additional internal reforms to its organisation and working methods that resulted in greater efficiencies and stronger governance despite the extent of its work being frequently widened in that period.

Among others, these reforms include audit (including the establishment of the internal audit function); the ethics function; the data protection officer; the annual conversation with Ambassadors; as well as a number of reports such as the Secretary-General's Management Report and the Value for Money report.

The Organisation's increased and varied membership, with its emphasis upon consensus, meant that it often took a lengthy period of time before proposed internal reforms could be agreed and implemented. This was not always the case however, as can be seen in its response to the COVID-19 pandemic, where the OECD rapidly shifted to fully virtual functioning, with thousands of virtual meetings, both internally and externally, as it continued with its operations.

3 From the Cold War to the OECD's 50th Anniversary

The Organisation for European Economic Co-operation (OEEC) was established in 1948 to supervise the US-financed Marshall Plan for the reconstruction of Europe following World War 2. The OEEC paved the way for a new era of co-operation and led to the signing of the Organisation for Economic Co-operation and Development (OECD) Convention on 14 December 1960. The Convention entered into force on 30 September 1961, marking the 'birth' of the OECD.

The OECD was born at the height of the Cold War. It was a time when continued economic growth was seen as vital for facing the Soviet threat, but was endangered by differing conceptions among its Members as to how integration in Western Europe should proceed. This chapter describes a number of the OECD's main developments during the first 50 years of its existence.[1]

From the OEEC to the OECD: The OECD in the 1960s

Article 3 of the OECD Convention makes monitoring economic trends, data collection, information sharing, policy analysis and consultation central aspects of the work of the OECD, usually drawn from the national statistics provided by Members. Based initially on much of the work done by the OEEC, especially as regards National Accounts data, the Economics and Statistics Department was successful in developing a strong reputation for this work, the standardisation and comparison of data, and the OECD Economic Surveys of each Member that resulted. The Department also helped economic growth to become a dominant policy goal for OECD governments at the first Ministerial Council Meeting (MCM) in November 1961, after vigorous debate, aiming at an ambitious increase in the combined GNP of Members by 50% over the next 10 years.

---

[1] Lack of space precludes detailed consideration of all OECD developments, but much can be found in Carroll, P, Kellow, A, 2011. *The OECD A study of Organisational Adaptation*, Edward Elgar, Cheltenham; Kellow, A, Carroll, P, 2017. *Middle Powers and International Organisations – Australia and the OECD*, Edward Elgar, Cheltenham; Leimgruber, M, Schmelzer, M (eds.), 2017. *The OECD and the International Political Economy Since 1948*, Palgrave Macmillan, Cham; Mahon, R, McBride, S (eds.), 2008. *The OECD and Transnational Governance*, UBC Press, Vancouver; Martens, K, Jakobi, A (eds.), 2010. *Mechanisms of OECD Governance*, Oxford University Press, Oxford; Pal, L, 2012. *Frontiers of Governance: The OECD and Global Public Management Reform*, Palgrave Macmillan, Cham; Schmelzer, M, 2016. *The Hegemony of Growth: The OECD and the Making of the Economic Growth Paradigm*, Cambridge University Press, Cambridge; Woodward, R, 2009. *The Organisation for Economic Co-operation and Development (OECD)*, Routledge, London.

https://doi.org/10.1515/9783110735833-003

The new Economic Policy Committee's key purpose at this time, and later, was to allow major, and often influential, treasury and finance officials gain an understanding of, and at least some sympathy with, the problems and attitudes of their counterparts in the other OECD Member governments. The Committee created two Working Parties, one being the influential Working Party 3 (WP3), specialising in the 1960s in sensitive, balance of payments international monetary issues and capital markets, with a restricted membership. Emile van Lennep was WP3's first chair and later became the OECD's second Secretary-General. As the international monetary system moved towards a flexible exchange rate regime in the 1970s, WP3's influence declined.

Global Relations, Japanese, Finnish, Australian and New Zealand Membership

The importance of an interdependent world outside its membership had been a continuing focus of the OEEC from its inception, with priority given to the UN and its specialised agencies, notably the IMF. However, the UN's declining status in the eyes of OECD Members is reflected in the OECD Convention, which makes no mention of the UN or the specialised agencies, although relationships with GATT, the IMF and the World Bank were maintained, though sometimes strained. Relationships with the European Economic Community (EEC) and European Free Trade Association (EFTA) were important, with both afforded privileged access to the OECD. The relationship with the EEC was however initially difficult, due to the complications of their overlapping memberships, but it became more positive as the decades passed.

In the early years of the OECD, there was no widespread, consistent demand by Members to expand membership, nor were there widespread requests to join. The exceptions were Japan, strongly supported by the USA, which gained membership in 1964, and Finland, with its challenging relationship with the USSR, that joined in January 1969, Australia in 1971 and New Zealand in 1973.

In addition to growing economic interdependence and the need to generate, maintain and enhance relations with both Members and non-members, the OECD makes it clear that external, global relations are of major importance. A principal motive for building its 'global relations' was, and is, to promote its views as to what should be the 'principles, values and policies that lead to sound, sustainable growth and poverty reduction'.

Trade and the Codes of Liberalisation

Trade and investment have been core focus areas of the OECD since its inception. The OECD has been promoting progressive liberalisation of current and capital account operations among its Members for 60 years. The work commenced when OEEC Members agreed that the high tariffs, quantitative restrictions on imports and various restrictions on the convertibility of currencies that were common in the 1940s should be gradually abolished, and developed a Code of Liberalisation of Trade (1950) and a Code of Liberalisation of Capital Movements (1959) to guide their efforts. The Codes were, and remain, legally binding instruments, obliging Members to maintain their existing degree of freedom for international capital movements and current invisible operations and to pursue further liberalisation in both areas.

In the negotiations leading up to the establishment of the OECD, the OEEC Members held widely differing views as to whether or not the new organisation should have any responsibilities in relation to trade. Despite persistent differences, OECD Members adopted and modified the two Codes, which provided a flexible framework for:
– Notifications by Members of related developments
– Examination of proposed or actual developments related to the Codes
– Consultations in which observance of the Codes was monitored

Initially, the Committee on Invisible Transactions (CIT) administered the Codes and, unusually, it consisted of experts nominated by Members but selected by Council, serving in a personal capacity, and its decisions could be made on the basis of a simple majority vote. Nearly all Members maintained some controls on external capital flows during the 1960s, as they were permitted to do under the Codes, although they were expected to explain and justify their retention. Given differences between Members, and the OECD's consensus rule, progress on liberalisation was slow in the 1960s, although it was to accelerate in later years, remaining a central feature of the Organisation.

Development and DAC

The OECD, as proposed by the USA, placed an increased focus on development, establishing the Development Assistance Committee (DAC) in 1960, followed by the Development Centre. The DAC concentrated initially on designing a comprehensive and comparable system for reporting and analysing statistics regarding development assistance, followed shortly by regular peer reviews of Members' aid policies and programmes, commencing in 1962.

The DAC had a restricted membership and, unusually, a full-time Chair appointed by its members, with a considerable degree of independence. The Chair was initially funded by the USA, although its incumbent, while usually American, was not appointed as a national representative and relied heavily upon the support of a new Development Directorate.

Among its achievements in the 1960s were the 1963 Resolution on the Terms and Conditions of Aid, and the 1965 Recommendation on Financial Terms and Conditions, which aimed to soften the financial conditions attached to development loans and grants. In 1966, Council approved DAC's proposal for the introduction of a joint OECD–World Bank reporting system on external lending, later to become the Creditor Reporting System, which provided the only detailed, comparative, up-to-date source of such data.

The question of what constituted aid, as opposed to concessional loans, was strongly contested in the DAC. In 1969 it adopted the concept of official development assistance (ODA). This was defined as official transactions with the main objective of promoting the economic and social development of developing countries. It came to be the international yardstick by which the generosity of aid was measured.

Economic Influence, the Oil Crises and the Rise of the Environment in the 1970s

The 1970s saw the end of the Bretton Woods system, recession and rising rates of inflation in most OECD Members' economies. This was exacerbated by the oil crises of 1973–1974 and 1979, developments that had a significant impact on many aspects of the work of the OECD, with its focus on economic issues. It placed energy very firmly on its agenda, with the establishment of the International Energy Agency in 1974 at the suggestion of the US Secretary of State Henry Kissinger. These developments also called for effective, international co-operation between the major states. However, growing economic policy disagreements, especially between the USA and several West European states, were evident in the IMF's Group of 10 (G10) and the WP3, each with a majority of European members. The UK, Denmark and Ireland joined the European Community in 1973, further consolidating the influence of the European Members of the OECD.

The result of continuing economic policy differences was the US-inspired creation of the G7 in 1976. This new and exclusive grouping sent a clear message of dissatisfaction with the value of the Bretton Woods institutions and the OECD. The G7 indicated a decline in the OECD's influence in international monetary and financial discussions. Key discussions previously held at the OECD increasingly shifted to the G7, where the OECD Secretariat was not invited and not informed, at least directly. Secretary-General van Lennep later wrote that the creation of the G7 had harmed the OECD and undermined its influence.

On the more positive side, the OECD played an important role in increasing the influence on policy developments of monetarist, flexible exchange rate approaches to economic policy, particularly with its 1977 publication of the McCracken Report (OECD, 1977a). The report was also an important influence on the adoption by the Ministerial Council of a strategy for sustained expansion, together with a series of action policies to assist in its implementation.

The Multinational Enterprise Guidelines

The OECD investment instruments grew out of the strong, often adverse, reaction by several developed and developing countries to the increasing growth and power of multinational enterprises (MNEs) in several OECD countries and the developing world during the late 1960s and early 1970s.

The key concern of many governments was how to manage foreign direct investment (FDI) and MNEs in an appropriate fashion. OECD governments were constrained by the fact that the OECD's Convention (Article 2d) specified that Members agreed 'to reduce or abolish obstacles to the exchange of goods and services and current payments and maintain and extend the liberalisation of capital movements'. These activities were monitored closely by the Committee for Invisible Transactions.

This complex issue was discussed at length and resulted in the 1976 OECD Declaration on International Investment and Multinational Enterprises that included the OECD Guidelines for Multinational Enterprises. The Guidelines are recommendations providing principles and standards of good practice consistent with applicable laws and internationally recognised standards. While substantially revised and expanded in later years, the Guidelines were the first intergovernmental code of conduct involving developed countries and were regarded as a substantial step forward in regulating the behaviour of MNEs.

International Tax Policy and Transfer Pricing

Work on tax goes back to the OEEC. The first major output of the OECD was the 'Draft Double Taxation Convention on Income and on Capital' in 1963. The Fiscal Committee was then asked to draft a convention to provide a mechanism for settling issues related to the double taxation of estates and inheritances, the 'Draft Convention for the Avoidance of Double Taxation with Respect to Taxes on Estates and Inheritances', published in 1966. The Convention has been remarkably influential, with an estimated 2,000 bilateral tax treaties having been based on it. It was followed by the OECD Transfer Pricing Guidelines for Multinational Enterprises and Tax Administrations (TPG), voluntary in nature, which have been regularly updated, most recently in the context of the OECD/G20 Inclusive Framework on Base Erosion and Profit Shifting (BEPS).

The TPG have become something of a 'bible', both for businesses and tax administrations, providing a set of transfer pricing rules that help ensure that transfer prices are not unrealistic and that profits, and their associated national tax revenues, are not moved from the jurisdiction where the value has been created. Increasingly, they have replaced or complemented national transfer pricing systems.

Trade and Export Credits

During the 1970s, the OECD's work on trade took on greater importance when the Council appointed a high-level committee under Jean Rey, a former President of the EEC Commission, to report on trade and related issues in a long-term perspective (OECD 1972). It was considered that there had been a substantial weakening of the General Agreement on Tariffs and Trade (GATT, now the World Trade Organisation) regime.

The Rey Committee's work provided a valuable basis for the Tokyo Round of GATT negotiations (1973–1979), although the only outcome was, following prompting by the US, an informal agreement among the industrialised nations to assess services in more detail in the OECD. Until then, governments had little explicit policy on services and there was little data regarding the significance of services trade, although it was becoming an increasingly important part of the economies of the OECD Members, and US multinationals were rapidly expanding their trade in services.

The OECD's work on export credits came to prominence in the 1970s. The bulk of such credit is provided by governments, particularly those of the richer, more developed economies, in the form of officially supported export credit for exporters competing for overseas sales, usually via a public agency or, indirectly, via a state-supported private sector agency. The terms offered for export credit are an important factor in determining which country's exporting firms are selected for purchases by overseas clients, so that export credit that is subsidised by governments provides an exporting firm with a competitive advantage. The increasing subsidies provided by governments led to growing concern and, in 1963 the OECD's Trade Committee established the Group on Export Credits and Credit Guarantees (ECG), initially a rather secretive body, to attempt to manage competition by agreeing a set of guidelines for export credit and to assess national policies.

Discussions moved very slowly, at first focusing on procedures for the exchange of information and it was not until 1978 that 'The Arrangement on Guidelines for Officially Supported Export Credits' was put in place, spurred on by the first oil shock. The Arrangement was not a formal OECD legal instrument as it was not agreed by the OECD Council, but a voluntary agreement, or 'soft law'. It applied only to official export credit with repayment terms of two years or more and excluded a number of sectors, notably agriculture. It also provided a set of rules as to how official support could be given.

Pollution, the Environment, and the Emerging Work on Social Indicators

Concerns for the natural environment emerged relatively slowly in the OECD. From the mid-1960s delegates began to raise the environmental concerns of their governments and the Organisation's work began to include a 'coherent environmental component' and to address the so-called 'problems of modern society', as identified in reports to the Science Policy Committee. The focus was on science relating to environmental threats and technologies for assessing and monitoring them, with the initial priorities being: pesticides and PCBs in water; urban air quality; transportation and noise; and watershed management.

An Environment Committee was established in 1970, serviced by an Environment Directorate – a first among international organisations – to promote the integration of environmental and economic policies, producing work that would reduce pollution, assess environmental performance, develop environmental protection tools, and improve international data and information on environmental issues. The OECD Secretariat also participated in the Club of Rome and its seminal 1972 report "Limits to Growth".

The Stockholm Environment Conference of 1972 also stimulated further action in the OECD. The ability of the OECD to establish conceptual frameworks that have broader implications was exemplified by early work on a Recommendation for a set of OECD Guiding Principles Concerning the International Economic Aspects of Environmental Policies in May 1972.

The best known of these was the 'Polluter Pays Principle', setting out the idea that polluters be charged for the costs of their action, which has had a significant impact on policy worldwide. Moreover, in 1974 the OECD developed principles dealing with transboundary pollution, interpreting and extending what had been agreed to in the Stockholm Declaration. The OECD also designed much of the policy architecture that was later used to develop the Basel Convention governing trade in hazardous waste.

The early 1970s also saw a lively debate emerge on the role of GDP as a measure of progress and well-being. This led to OECD Ministers approving in May 1973 a list of social concerns common to most OECD countries. The economic crisis that followed the 1973–1974 oil shock effectively shifted the focus back to growth and jobs.

Decline and Success: The Challenges of the 1980s

The 1980s commenced with continuing inflation and the worst recession since 1945, accompanied by increased protectionism. OECD economies struggled to cope with what was described as 'stagflation', where excess capacity and unemployment, combined with inflation, resulted in little or no economic growth. The recovery began in 1983, together with the growing influence of supply-side economics, focusing on the need to lower taxes and decrease regulation. The decade also witnessed the beginning of the end of the Cold War, the rise to prominence of environmental issues and the signing of the Single European Act in 1986, expanding the role of the European Commission and bringing about major institutional reform in what became the European Union. Much of the OECD's work focused on the analysis of these issues and on a series of attempts to gain agreements among its Members as to appropriate, concerted policy responses.

Positive Adjustment

The creation of the G7 in the 1970s had seen a reduction in the influence of the OECD in international economic policy coordination, so that by the 1980s it was only one of a range of international organisations that could be used for the implementation of agreements made in the G7, and for the monitoring of compliance. However, it still provided a forum in which its Members, notably those in the G7, could develop actions aimed at monetary stabilisation and economic growth. It also provided credible and influential analysis to support proposals for action.

Nevertheless, as David Henderson, a former head of the OECD's Economics Department, noted:

> . . . too much should not be expected of it. It is not a substitute for well-chosen domestic policies. Its role is to build on and reinforce such policies, the responsibility for which remains with national governments.[2]

Positive or structural adjustment became increasingly important in the OECD in the 1980s. In summary, it emphasised the need to rely predominantly on market forces in the formulation of economic policy. The Special Group of the OECD's Economic Policy Committee increasingly recommended national programmes of adjustment, or microeconomic reform, that aimed at reducing or eliminating the benefits that had accrued to business and/or worker interests on the basis of earlier, often protectionist, economic policies in the 1950s and 1960s. Perhaps the most influential of the OECD reports resulting from this body of work was the 1987 'Structural Adjustment and Economic Performance' report, which provided a conceptual basis for a wide range of microeconomic and regulatory reform studies and related recommendations that characterised the work of the OECD in the 1990s. In a very real sense the adjustment programmes, where adopted by members, represented a growing influence by the OECD on Members' domestic economic policy.

Agriculture

The increasing influence of supply-side economics and positive adjustment was also felt in the OECD's work on agriculture, in the context of the increasing cost of the EU's

---

2 Henderson, D. (1993), 'International economic cooperation re-visited', *Government and Opposition*, 28, 11–35.

contentious Common Agricultural Policy (CAP), with several Members adopting pro-grammes of reform that aimed to open up their agricultural sectors to greater, market-based, competition. These were reforms guided, in part, by the research and related publications of the OECD's Trade and Agriculture Directorates, which found slowly in-creasing sympathy among officials of the European Commission. The OECD's further elaboration of the concept and measurement of producer subsidy equivalents (PSE), followed later by the consumer subsidy equivalent (CSE), was particularly important, and was adopted by the OECD in the 1982 Ministerial Trade Mandate.

The concept was developed to provide a common measure of the cost of the wide range of differing types of government support for agriculture offered by OECD Members to their farmers. The PSE offered a more accurate and, importantly, com-parative accounting of the real costs of agricultural support in Member states. In turn, especially in the EU, it enabled more objective bargaining among EU and non-EU Member governments in the OECD and also within the WTO about the real extent of subsidies in agricultural policies and their impact.

The End of the Cold War and the Search for a More Global Role in a Competitive Environment: The Stirrings of Reform in the 1990s

The end of the Cold War, while welcome, faced the OECD with a number of chal-lenges, including what assistance, if any, it should provide to Eastern Europe and Russia, and whether the countries involved should be admitted to OECD member-ship. Questions regarding the Organisation's very existence also arose, given the end – it was thought – of the political and economic tensions that had accompanied the Cold War, while the second half of the 1990s also witnessed sharp cutbacks in its budget and declining staff morale.

Despite such challenges, the Organisation moved ahead with what became glob-ally important work on tax, education and the Convention on Combating Bribery of Foreign Public Officials in International Business Transactions (the Anti-Bribery Con-vention). In contrast, its pioneering work in developing the Multilateral Agreement on Investment was not successful.

The End of the Cold War and New Members

After the accession of New Zealand in 1973, there was little discussion of enlarge-ment by Members until it was stimulated by the end of the Cold War. After difficult discussions, in 1991 it was agreed that only Czechoslovakia, Hungary and Poland would be offered the opportunity of membership. This cautious approach was some-thing of a compromise between the views of its non-European (USA, Canada, Japan, Australia and New Zealand) and European members. The former argued that the

Organisation should not become even more dominated by its European members, most of whom were also Members of the increasingly influential EU. The compromise included offering the possibility of membership to Mexico and South Korea, with Mexico acceding in 1994 (and to NAFTA in the same year), the Czech Republic and Poland in 1995, Hungary and South Korea in 1996, and the Slovak Republic in 2000.

As well as the cautious approach to enlargement, in the later 1980s and into the 1990s, the OECD increased its engagement with a range of other countries, including Russia in 1992, China in 1996 and Brazil in 1998. Some, such as Mexico, had become observers at one or more OECD committees from the 1970s, with Mexico's privatisation programme and trade reforms following its 1982 debt crisis being highly regarded, helping pave the way to its accession in 1994. Angel Gurría, then Mexico's Foreign Affairs Minister and later to become the OECD's Secretary-General, played an important role in supporting Mexico's accession.

Intensifying Work on Tax

Tax work intensified and broadened in the late 1980s. Concerns emerged that some Member countries had adopted legislation that overrode the provisions of all or some of the double taxation treaties, so the OECD therefore developed a Recommendation requesting Members to undertake consultations with treaty partners when problems arose, and to avoid adopting legislation in contradiction of treaty obligations. It also instructed the (now) Committee on Fiscal Affairs to monitor the situation and notify the Council of any material breaches of tax treaties by Member states.

The Challenge of MAI

The relatively private nature of proceedings in the OECD became an issue in 1995, when the Organisation sought to develop a Multilateral Agreement on Investment (MAI) whose aim was to liberalise foreign investment by Member countries. It proposed that Members should not discriminate between rules for foreign and domestic investors. NGOs however – their concerns amplified by the secrecy surrounding the negotiations – feared that the MAI would undermine the ability of Members to undertake environmental, social or consumer regulation. Negotiations were approved at the MCM in May 1995 and commenced in September 1995, but were abandoned in 1998 after a largely internet-based NGO campaign that rocked the OECD. In response, the OECD became a more open Organisation, consulting more with social and environmental NGOs.

The Anti-Bribery Convention: Dealing with Bribery and Corruption

The years leading to the end of the Cold War also saw rapidly increasing international trade, often accompanied by increasing corruption, as noted by Transparency International. Moreover, the 1976 OECD Guidelines for Multinational Enterprises, which encouraged companies to refrain from bribery in their business dealings, were having little or no impact in this context. The end of the Cold War and the increasing loss of lucrative contracts by US companies led US governments to argue, repeatedly, for stronger OECD action in relation to bribery. This resulted in a number of important developments. The first was the 1994 OECD Recommendation on Bribery in International Business Transactions, requesting Members to examine the adequacy of their existing legislation regarding bribery; and to report back on the impact of their anti-bribery and corruption regimes. This was strengthened by the 1996 Recommendation on the Tax Deductibility of Bribes to Foreign Public Officials, aimed at the ending of such deductibility and instructing the Committee on Fiscal Affairs, in co-operation with the Committee on International Investment and Multinational Enterprises, to monitor the implementation of the Recommendation.

Following a review of the impact of these developments, the 1997 Convention on Combatting Bribery of Foreign Public Officials in International Business Transactions was agreed. Signed by all 29 Members and 5 non-members, signatories agreed to criminalise all types of illicit payments made across national borders to public officials.

INES and PISA

From the 1970s onwards, the OECD's work on education was amplified, in particular through the OECD Centre for Educational Research and Innovation (CERI) which was established in 1968 with the financial support of the Ford Foundation and Royal Dutch Shell. CERI was notable for its development of the Indicators of Educational Systems Programme (INES), which commenced in 1988, and addresses many of the technical aspects related to OECD education activities. Today, CERI develops and analyses indicators and data collection instruments for all levels of education, notably through its *'Education at A Glance'* (EAG) report, which has been produced annually since 1992.

In 1997, the OECD launched the Programme for International Student Assessment (PISA), an international survey. Conducted triennially on 15-year-old students. PISA's first survey took place in 2000 with 43 countries participating and it has since been expanded in scope to include a large number of non-OECD Members – PISA 2018 included 79 countries. PISA has substantial influence and is a response to countries' desire for high quality and regular data on both the knowledge and skills of their students and the performance of their education systems. More than

500,000 students participate in the PISA survey, and are tested on reading, mathematics and science. In total, 44 'economies' (including places like Hong Kong, Shanghai and Chinese Taipei) take part.

From Johnston to Gurría: The Reforms of the 2000s

The dawn of a new century saw the OECD faced with many of the same challenges it had faced in the 1990s. For example, the economies of its Members continued to experience a decline in their share of the global economy, thanks to globalisation and the emergence of China, India, Brazil, Russia and other developing countries. Similarly, the EU continued to grow in importance, as did its Members within the OECD. Internal reforms to structures and processes, begun slowly in the 1990s, gathered pace. In this context, the OECD chose to continue to expand its role with a policy of increased membership and enhanced engagement with new partners.

Global Relations: Further Accession and Enhanced Engagement

The accessions of Mexico, Korea and the eastern European Members had extended the international reach of the Organisation in the 1990s, but the development of the 'Asian tigers' and, in particular, the emergence of China and India meant that the OECD share of both global economic output and trade was rapidly diminishing. Hence, in 2003, the OECD established a working group under the Japanese Ambassador Seiichiro Noboru to develop a formal strategy for enlargement and co-operation with non-members.

The working group developed four criteria for considering the suitability of states for membership: there had to be 'like-mindedness'; the state had to be a 'significant player'; there needed to be 'mutual benefit' from membership; and there had to be regard given to 'global considerations', particularly keeping some sort of agreed 'balance' between European and non-European members. The working group's recommendations were agreed at the 2004 MCM, and in 2007 Council agreed to open accession discussions with Chile, Estonia, Israel, the Russian Federation and Slovenia. The OECD Committees assessed each candidate country's capacity to implement the OECD legal instruments and compared their existing policies and practices to those of the OECD.

In addition, it was decided to strengthen co-operation with Brazil, China, India, Indonesia and South Africa (now known as 'key partners'), through a process of 'enhanced engagement', with the possibility that they might eventually become full members. A similar process of closer engagement was also increasingly emphasised with a number of regions, notably South East Asia, Latin America and the Caribbean, the Middle East and North Africa.

From Tax Havens to BEPS

The G8 meeting in Lyon in 1996 referred to the OECD the matter of 'harmful tax competition' (HTC). The initial effort in this area was not a success, but, later, circumstances and entrepreneurship on the part of Secretary-General Gurría eventually gave rise to improved outcomes. The Committee on Fiscal Affairs produced a report, *Harmful Tax Competition: An Emerging Global Issue*, in April 1998. The Report identified two types of HTC: tax havens and preferential tax regimes (PTRs). The Council adopted the recommendations, but Switzerland and Luxembourg (considered as tax havens) abstained from the Council Decision, meaning that they were not bound by the Decision. The balance of the Members agreed to eradicate their harmful PTRs within five years, review their own regimes and report any instances of harmful tax practices to a Forum on Harmful Tax Practices established by the Decision.

In 2008, 17 countries, led by France and Germany, proposed a blacklist of tax havens. Switzerland and Luxembourg boycotted the meeting, while the US and Austria also declined to send representatives. Germany, France and other countries called on the OECD specifically to add Switzerland to the blacklist of countries that encouraged tax fraud.

Following the election of the Obama US administration in November 2008, and continued calls from the G8 and G20, the four OECD countries (Austria, Belgium, Luxembourg and Switzerland) that had opposed the OECD standard dropped their opposition. Then in 2012, the OECD, with the support of the G20, launched a project on Base Erosion and Profit Shifting (BEPS) to recommend further adjustments to the international tax system.

The OECD and the Global Financial Crisis

The OECD experienced both failure and success in relation to the global financial crisis. Its failure, as with the BIS and the IMF, was that it did not notice the need for monetary tightening, the weak capital base and the lack of resilience of the banking systems in major economies, despite its responsibility for surveillance of macroeconomic and structural policies to promote economic prosperity for Members and non-members. Its forecasting also proved inaccurate, as it had been in the early 1970s oil crisis, tending to overestimate growth, which was also the case for the IMF and the European Commission.

However, on the positive side, the OECD rapidly introduced a range of improvements to its forecasting and analytical methods, especially short-term forecasting, with a greater focus on financial market developments and risk assessments. It also rapidly developed a systematic, strategic response to the crisis, incorporating a range of actions by Members and non-members, policy recommendations, and, as noted above, improved and extended surveillance activities. Thanks to Secretary-General

Gurría's intervention, the OECD was formally invited to attend G20 meetings starting with the Pittsburgh Summit in September 2009. The Secretary-General was also invited to appoint a Sherpa (Gabriela Ramos).

In addition, following extensive and successful lobbying by Secretary-General Gurría, the OECD was able to secure the G20 Leaders endorsement for its tax information exchange agenda in 2009 and later requests for further work on a range of additional policy areas. In essence, given the G20's lack of a secretariat, developing and implementing detailed policy prescriptions required co-operation from leading international organisations such as the OECD, which had a particularly wide range of expertise across a similarly wide range of policy areas.

Conclusion

The OECD has proved a remarkably active and adaptable organisation since its creation, developing an expanding range of largely 'soft law', conventions and standards for its Members that, increasingly, are also being adopted by non-members on a global basis. As well as its largely successful outputs, the last two decades have seen substantial reforms to its budgeting, auditing and human resource systems, often despite considerable opposition, but driven forward to a successful conclusion in the Gurría years. It is now well-placed to continue its expanding, global role into the future.

4 Leadership

In the past 15 years, up until May 2021, Secretary-General Gurría has led a wide range of organisational, policy and process reforms at the OECD, the widest range of reforms initiated by any Secretary-General in the OECD's history. Several of the reforms he instituted were stimulated, at least in part, by the global financial crisis (GFC) of 2008, and supported by the increased administrative capacity his internal reforms to the OECD provided. The achievements were not only the result of the energetic Secretary-General, but the support provided by a highly-qualified, experienced and hard-working staff, both in his Office (which was reorganised shortly after he took up his duties) and in the Directorates and Centres that he leads.

In most of the many interviews undertaken for this book, the individuals that make up the staff of the OECD, as well as a range of Ambassadors, frequently praised the leadership of the Secretary-General, his clear and consistent vision for the Organisation in which they worked, his ability to draw out the best in them, his courage in dealing with challenging situations, and his sense of humour and vivacity, the latter being qualities not all leaders possess. This chapter is largely about the Secretary-General, a figure too often neglected in studies of the OECD, but vital for its operations and success.

The Candidate

Gurría's views in relation to the OECD and its future began to emerge and develop well before his candidacy for the position of Secretary-General, particularly in regard to its enlargement. He was part of the team that negotiated Mexico's accession to the OECD in 1994, and developed close relations with the Organisation when he was Mexico's Minister for Foreign Affairs, from December 1994 to January 1998, and then as Minister of Finance from 1998 to 2000. In all of these roles he gained a detailed understanding of the OECD and its work, as well as a growing affection for the Organisation and an increasing range of useful contacts.

He was sympathetic with the goal of enlargement of membership and had made moves in this direction in 1999, when, as Mexico's Finance Minister, he chaired the OECD's Ministerial Council Meeting (MCM). At his initiative, a number of emerging and developing countries were invited for the first time to participate at this meeting in a dialogue with OECD countries on a range of policy issues.

Gurría was also keen during his candidacy to improve what he and several others felt was the Organisation's relatively obscure and declining profile, suggesting it could become a secretariat of the globalisation process, so that when the OECD made proposals, gave an opinion, or suggested best practices, the public and political elites would pay attention. In particular, he felt that it could become a permanent

https://doi.org/10.1515/9783110735833-004

advisory body or secretariat to the G7/G8 and the recently formed G20 (pre-GFC), with which he had become familiar as Mexico's Minister of Finance.

In practice, the OECD was already partially fulfilling the role of a secretariat for the G8 in regard to a growing, but fluctuating range of issues, though its members showed little or no desire for this role to be made permanent, nor for the OECD to occupy it. At the 1996 G7 Lyon Summit, the OECD was urged to vigorously pursue its work, on a multilateral basis, to limit harmful tax competition and the erosion of national tax bases. At the 1999 G8 Cologne Summit, Members asked the OECD to undertake a range of tasks and to report back to the G8 at its next Summit.

Gurría also stressed the need to view social cohesion as a central goal of economic policy, to extend the benefits of social and economic progress to millions of citizens by reducing unemployment and providing adequate safety nets. He went on to note that the ultimate goal of policies is not just to promote economic growth, but, above all, social well-being. This view came to fruition in the work on well-being and inclusive growth that he consistently championed during his tenure at the OECD.

In his interview for the position, Gurría stated his initial three priorities. The first was to boost OECD's work on health, work that had received increasing attention and considerable praise during the three-year Health Project, as noted in Chapter 12 of this book. The second was to give a greater priority to work on migration, a topic of major and growing concern, this priority was thus not surprising. Gurría was aware that the OECD had been involved in work on migration from the 1960s (the OECD's International Migration Outlook, for example, is now in its 44th yearly edition), increasing in the 1990s in response to Council urgings as the economic and social significance of migration became clearer, and concern grew over the rapid rise of illegal migration to Europe. Further, in 2001 the International Organisation for Migration (IOM) had launched the International Dialogue on Migration, aiming to increase cooperation between it and other international organisations such as the OECD. In 2003 the UN had established a Global Commission on International Migration to develop policy recommendations, and in 2006 the High-Level Dialogue at the General Assembly focused on international migration for the first time.

His third priority, water governance and economics, came as something of a surprise to OECD Ambassadors, for it was not at that time treated as a major issue at the Organisation. Gurría, however, had become acutely aware of its growing importance while a minister in Mexico, given the acute water shortages in the north of the country, and became increasingly involved in international work in the area, actively contributing to the Camdessus Report (World Panel on Financing Water Infrastructure, 2003) and joining the United Nations Secretary-General's Advisory Board on Water and Sanitation. In 2006, shortly after his appointment as Secretary-General, he chaired the Water Financing Taskforce at the 4th World Water Forum, held in Mexico.

Gurría's appointment as Secretary-General rested, in part, on the close alignment of these and other views with those of the Council in 2005, together with its desire for an assertive leader and communicator who had not only broad international experience and proven leadership qualities, but an ability 'to enhance the competence and global influence of the organisation', and to 'represent the OECD at the highest level with governments, other stakeholders and academic institutions'. Gurría exhibited all of these qualities and, in addition, his appointment as the first Secretary-General from Mexico sent a clear signal to non-members that the OECD was becoming a more open, though still exclusive club.

Settling in and Getting it Right: 2006–2007

The early days of Gurría's tenure were challenging as he began the task of learning about the OECD in more detail, not easy given the wide and increasing range of subject areas in which the Organisation was involved, as well as the sheer volume of reports it produced. In addition, he was faced with a number of recently approved reforms that required implementation, as well as a number of still to be completed reviews and related reforms, notably the full implementation of the new Integrated Management Cycle (IMC), a review of Human Resource Management (HRM) policies and practices, and a review of internal controls.

He was also faced with continuing budget pressures and the recent, important decision of Council to launch a process to expand the OECD's global reach and policy impact through an enlarged membership and enhanced engagement with non-members. This engagement was to use the criteria outlined in the 2004, 'Noboru Report', (significant player, mutual benefit, like-mindedness, and global considerations) as a basis for a more detailed accession process, and to assess potential accession candidates. Council required the new Secretary-General to identify countries for potential accession, and countries for enhanced engagement with the OECD, by the end of July 2006, only two months after he came to office.

In this demanding context, Gurría proceeded cautiously, not only because of the time it took to master the Organisation's complexities, but because of his respect for its highly qualified and experienced staff, who were not likely to greet demands for sudden and dramatic reform from a Secretary-General still feeling his way with any great enthusiasm. Nevertheless, as noted below, the range of reforms completed and initiated in his early months were substantial.

Implementing and Completing Reforms Underway

The new Secretary-General made it clear that among his priorities in his first, consolidated proposal regarding budget assumptions and priorities for the 2007–2008 biennium, would be the achievement of financial reforms aimed at putting the OECD on a secure financial basis for the next 10 years (in contrast to the previous 10 years of cutbacks); and completion of the major reviews of human resource management, budgeting and financial management policies and systems launched by his predecessor, Secretary-General Johnston. A further, recently completed review was undertaken by Council's Budget Committee to ensure that the full cost of projects funded by the rapidly growing use of voluntary contributions was charged to those projects. This proved an ongoing issue and further reforms were approved by Council in 2008, which noted that changes to the approved Programme of Work and Budget (PWB) often resulted from the receipt of additional voluntary contributions during the biennium, making Council control and accountability of such contributions a continuing challenge.

Gurría stressed to Council that the current operations of the OECD, and several of his desired reforms, had been severely curtailed by continuing budget pressures, with the result that the Organisation had not operated at its full potential. The combined level of Part I Budget and voluntary contributions for 2005, for example, was below that available in 1992, and more than 11 per cent below that available in 1994. As he emphasised, this had had a negative impact on staff morale and enthusiasm, and would not be an adequate basis for reforms already in train, or his intended reforms.

After lengthy discussions, in June 2008 Council agreed to guarantee that for the next 10 years Part I funding would be maintained in real terms (i.e. adjusted for host-country inflation). In effect, it had agreed to Gurría's proposal to substitute the principle of zero real growth (ZRG) for the zero nominal growth (ZNG) of earlier years, a substantial achievement given the developing GFC. As a result, the OECD was initially shielded from the budget cuts suffered by other international organisations in this difficult period. However, Council later decided to treat only half of the Part II Programmes Budget to the ZRG assumption, with the other half subject to ZNG, so that by the proposed budget for 2019–2020, this latter part had been subject to ZNG constraint for 10 and 11 years, given the cumulative impact of inflation during these years. This was despite the fact that, for example, the agreed standards for tax information exchange developed by the OECD, had benefited Members by an estimated total of €66 billion, representing more than 330 times Members' Part I assessed contributions. The budgetary reforms, combined with revisions to the calculation of Members' Part I contributions, also helped persuade the US Administration to agree to proceed on the 2007 enlargement proposal, as its contributions fell from approximately 25% to 20.5% (2019), as the revisions were introduced. Members' contributions are based on both a proportion that is shared equally and a scale proportional to the relative size of their economies.

Budget constraints and their negative impact were a topic the Secretary-General returned to on a number of occasions. In regard to the 2018 proposals for the 2019–2020 budget, notwithstanding the considerable argument by the Secretary-General to persuade Members to return to the ZRG model for the 2021–2022 biennium, several members of Council successfully argued for a departure from the 2008 agreement for the automatic application of ZRG indexation to the budget and, in addition, to have the Organisation absorb the increased costs of staff pension contributions, despite the efficiencies gained from the Value for Money (V4M) programme. This cost the OECD an estimated 24 million Euros, which it had to absorb in its budget. It was only on the 2020–2021 Budget that inflation was again recognised, although Members still kept the additional pension payments as part of the OECD's budget for the biennium (4.3 million Euros) which undercut the work on substantive issues.

The HRM review was concluded at the end of 2006 and a comprehensive package of reforms was submitted to Council for consideration in January 2007, to be implemented over 2007–2010, enhancing the merit-based recruitment system. The aim was also to make HR policies more flexible within the context of the OECD's new, results-based planning, budgeting and management system, providing managers with increased responsibility and authority for management of staff and budgets, as well as improved accountability mechanisms and controls. The review of internal controls was completed and approved by Council in 2008, based largely on the Committee of Sponsoring Organisations of the Treadway Commission (COSO) 1992 model, a system supported by the International Organisation of Supreme Audit Institutions. While changes to the management of voluntary contributions were undertaken in 2008, improving the capacity of Budget Committee and Council to control their use, it continued to be a problem area, with a further review taking place in 2009.

Initiating Reforms

Gurría also took the opportunity in presenting his views on the 2007–2008 PWB to note that during his candidacy he had stated that his overriding objective would be to improve the relevance of the OECD, and that among his initial priorities to this end were:
- Additional resources for health, migration and water, which he had noted as priority areas during his candidacy and where he felt the OECD should seek to have greater global policy impact, even though neither migration or water had received significant support in the recent Medium Term Orientations Process (MTO) Survey.
- A need to strengthen capacity to respond to emerging and unforeseen demands by doubling the Secretary-General's Allocation Fund to €1.2 million, giving him greater resources for supporting priority areas running short of funds, as well as dealing with smaller scale emergencies.
- The review and improvement of the OECD website, regarded as a very high priority and a part of the Secretary-General's drive to lift the profile of the Organisation.
- Increased funding for outreach-related projects of €400,000 for 2007 and for 2008, as well as a review of global relations activities and their funding for the OECD as a whole, noting their growing importance and his commitment to their expansion.

- A €1 million provision for the launching of enlargement procedures and enhanced engagement with non-Members in the PWB, a high priority for both himself and Council. Increases in funding for global relations became common, especially after 2011 and Council's goal of the OECD becoming the centre of a global policy network. In the Secretary-General's PWB submission for 2011–2012, for example, there was a proposed increase for global relations-related and enhanced engagement outputs of 26% for the biennium.

As described in Chapter 12 of this book, his support for work on health was evident throughout his tenure, as was his support for work on water. He established a multidisciplinary water team soon after taking up office and the work of the team helped lead to the development of a set of OECD principles on water governance in 2015 and, in 2016, the Council recommendation on water. It also led to interorganisational projects such as the 2007 'Sustainable Financing to ensure affordable water and sanitation', involving the OECD's Environment, Agriculture, Investment and Development Committees, as well as the World Bank, the EU Water Initiative, and the UN Secretary-General's Advisory Board on Water and Sanitation (UNSGAB).

The priority Gurría gave to migration was in line with the long-established OECD interest in the subject, going back to the early years of the OEEC. While fluctuating in scope and intensity in the OECD, the end of the 1990s saw the growing interest of Council in international migration, with work being focused in the Directorate of Employment, Labour and Social Affairs (DELSA), the Economics Department, the Education Directorate (EDU) and the Development Centre (DEV). The added support of the new Secretary-General soon resulted in an increased output related to migration, such as the 2007–2008 review 'Jobs for Immigrants', the 2008 review on migrant education, the chapters on immigration in the country economic surveys, and the 2007 'Gaining from Migration', from DEV. As with other areas of the OECD's work, significant financial support has come from the European Commission, with its growing need for data and policy advice in relation to the rapidly increasing migration, legal and illegal, that its Members have faced.

Towards a Global Relations Strategy and Relations with the G8 and the G20

As described in Chapter 3, a new Strategy for Enlargement and Outreach was adopted by the MCM in 2005, becoming the precursor of the OECD's global relations strategy developed under Gurría in 2006–2007. Importantly, for the first time in the OECD's history, the Strategy included a systematic accession process for potential Members, with three key criteria for determining the eligibility of candidate countries: like-mindedness, being a significant player in the global economy and bringing an increased degree of global diversity to the Organisation's membership.

On taking up his position as Secretary-General on 1 June 2006, Gurría moved rapidly to promote the OECD as a 'hub of globalisation', a centre for discussion where Members and non-members could come together to find the tools necessary to better manage globalisation, which he saw as a 'fundamental new mission for the Organisation'.

Expanding Relations with the G8

The OECD had not been invited to attend as a participant at the G8's St Petersburg Summit, July 15–17, 2006, but the new Secretary-General immediately made clear his intent to promote the OECD not only as a 'hub' of globalisation but, in effect, as a secretariat for the G8 by attending the meeting of G8 education ministers in Moscow on 1–2 June, the first two days of his tenure as Secretary-General, when he might have been expected to be in Paris, introducing himself to OECD officials and ambassadors. This was followed by his attendance at the meeting of the G8 Labour and Employment Ministers in October, also in Moscow. In Moscow, he stressed the importance of the social dimension of globalisation and the relevance of the 2006 OECD Jobs Strategy, noting that it provided a benchmark on how countries could create more and better-paid jobs in a globalising world. In addition, in November 2006, a G8 International Conference on improving financial literacy was co-organised by Russia's Minister of Finance and the OECD, as part of the OECD's project on financial literacy, attended by several OECD officials and the OECD's Deputy Secretary-General Richard Hecklinger.

This rapidly emerging pattern of attendance at G7/G8 meetings by the Secretary-General, his Sherpa and occasionally his deputies, helped Gurría and the OECD cement closer relations with the G7/G8, which became very evident with the 2007 G8 Heiligendamm Summit, the first to which the OECD was officially invited to attend as a participant, a conspicuous success, providing Secretary-General Gurría with a substantially increased degree of access to the G8 leaders and, at least potentially, some influence over its work. At the Summit, the OECD agreed to provide a two year, 'platform for dialogue', between the G8 countries and Brazil, China, India, Mexico and South Africa (the G5), on four major topics: investment; innovation; development; energy efficiency. Described as the Heiligendamm Dialogue Process, its aim was to build trust and confidence among the dialogue partners and a common understanding of global issues. At the G8 Summit in Italy in 2009, it was agreed to continue this process under the name of the Heiligendamm L'Aquila Process (HAP). In July 2009, the OECD Council agreed to extend the mandate of the HAP Support Unit until the French Summit in 2011, following the submission of the concluding report by the HAP Support Unit, which had been under the direct supervision of Gurría, supported by his Chief of Staff.

This G8 drive to dialogue with the G5 at the 2005 Gleneagles Summit was very much in alignment with the OECD's new Global Relations Strategy (see Chapter 5 for details) under the leadership of Secretary-General Gurría, especially its enhanced engagement target countries, Brazil, China, India, Indonesia and South Africa; with Brazil, China, India and South Africa also being targeted by the G8. Indeed, the years 2007–2009 saw an increasingly active and successful involvement of the OECD with the G8 as Gurría and senior officials in his Office worked to promote the OECD's value and influence. In 2007, for example, the G8 members committed to intensifying their efforts to combat corruption by fully implementing their OECD agreements, and in 2008 at the L'Aquila Summit, the OECD received repeated acknowledgement and support for a wide range of its standards and principles that it had undertaken for the G8.

The success marked by the growing involvement of the OECD with the G8 was mirrored by the breaking of the stalemate in Council as regards the selection of candidates for accession and the enlargement of the OECD's membership. In summary, the breakthrough was achieved, in part, by gaining US agreement to advance on enlargement if a new agreement on member contributions to Part I of the budget also could be agreed, though such an agreement came later in 2008. In 2007, following Council discussions in which Gurría was heavily involved as chair, it was agreed that accession discussions would commence with Chile, Estonia, Israel, Slovenia and the Russian Federation.

It was also agreed that Gurría could inform other countries that had applied for membership that their applications would be considered as enlargement proceeded, as would future applications. The imprecise nature of this latter agreement was not greeted enthusiastically, but at least it signalled Council's willingness, however reluctant, to consider further enlargement.

Building and Maintaining Relations with the G20

The rapid rise of the G20 as the predominant focus of global economic governance following the GFC was something of a challenge for the OECD's Secretary-General as, while it contained 11 OECD Members and the EU, eight of its members were drawn from the developing world, with no reason to think highly of the OECD. However, the G8 members of the G20 finance ministers' meetings had received the OECD's rapidly growing support for their objectives in the previous two years, making them fully aware of the OECD's capacity to provide wide-ranging support for the G20 Leaders' meetings, as well as the growing range of the G20's specialised, ministerial meetings.

In addition, before the GFC, the G20 finance ministers had already requested the OECD to address the question of tax evasion, which led to its Agreement on Exchange of Information on Tax Matters, to which the finance ministers, both OECD and non-OECD members, committed themselves at the 2004 Berlin Summit. In 2008 the Agreement was also endorsed by the UN Committee of Experts on International

Cooperation in Tax Matters. The OECD then gradually increased its involvement with not only the G20 Finance Ministers meetings, but also with Agriculture, Labour and Employment Ministers' meetings.

Despite this record, the OECD was not invited to participate with global leaders in the first two G20 leaders' summits, in Washington and in London, although the World Bank, United Nations, IMF and Financial Stability Forum had been invited to send delegates. At the 2008 Washington meeting, while not attending, the OECD was encouraged to continue to promote its Agreement on the Exchange of Information for Tax Purposes. Gurría then contacted the UK Prime Minister, Gordon Brown, urging him to advance the tax agenda and, importantly, at the 2009 London Summit, chaired by Brown, the G20 Leaders made tax havens a high priority. They were also encouraged to do so by an OECD report issued on the final day of the Summit that demonstrated the need for further work on international tax and, of course the OECD as the primary source of the necessary expertise. Gurría was asked by Gordon Brown to stay in his office, 'even to sleep in your office', but be ready to send the report when requested. Other OECD officials were present in London.

It was in this context, with the G20 leaders increasingly aware of the need for organisational support in developing and implementing its widening range of agreements, especially if it was to maintain credibility, that Secretary-General Gurría and his senior officials saw an opportunity to reinforce the impact and influence of the OECD's reputation. He engaged in a surge of lobbying efforts with leaders in national capitals as to the usefulness of the OECD for the G20. In this regard, Gurría and his Chief of Staff, Gabriela Ramos' discussion with President Obama's newly appointed Sherpa Mike Froman, and Deputy Secretary-General Pier Carlo Padoan's relationship with European governments were particularly important.

The Secretary-General also directed the development within the Organisation of a range of reports tailored to the interests of G20 members, as well as working with the ILO, IMF, World Bank and the WTO to bring together the policy rules they had all developed into a single inventory. This was useful in promoting a new global consensus on the key values and principles of sustainable growth, a high priority of the G20. This work was endorsed by the G20 Leaders at their 2008 Washington Summit, where their 'Action Plan to Implement Principles for Reform', urged tax authorities to draw upon the work of bodies such as the OECD in continuing efforts to promote tax information exchange, further noting that a lack of transparency and a failure to exchange tax information should be 'vigorously addressed'.

These efforts soon bore fruit. The G20 Action Plan for Recovery and Reform developed and agreed at the 2009 London Summit, with the OECD's work on tax havens in mind, noted that Leaders would take action against non-cooperative jurisdictions, including tax havens, backed up by sanctions, and that the era of banking secrecy was over. Importantly, the Action Plan noted that the OECD 'has today published a list of countries assessed by the Global Forum against the international standard for exchange of tax information'.

The release on the 2 April 2009 of this 'list of countries', was the 'Progress Report on the Jurisdictions Surveyed by the OECD Global Forum in Implementing the Internationally Agreed Tax Standard'. Its release was a courageous move by the Secretary-General, for it had not been proposed, discussed or approved by the OECD Council. Legal advice was that it was not a wise move, and would upset, at the least, those OECD Members who received a negative assessment on the list, notably Austria, Belgium, Switzerland and Luxembourg. The advice was correct in that these four Members made their displeasure very clear. In contrast, the G20 members welcomed the Report, with its clear implications for their domestic constituencies that they were taking action to remedy at least a part of the weaknesses in the international financial system that had brought about the GFC. Also, if effective, the reduction in the adverse impact of tax havens would help to boost their tax revenues, much needed to help cover the costs of dealing with the GFC.

The combined impact of the Secretary-General's successful lobbying in 2008–2009, the value of the OECD's work in relation to tax, and the prospect of the OECD providing assistance to the growing range of the G20's work, saw the OECD formally invited, for the first time, to attend a G20 Summit, the one held in Pittsburgh in September 2009. While, as Gurría described it, the invitation was only a 'day pass' to this specific Summit, it was a day pass renewed for all following G20 Leaders' Summits, a sign of the continuing value placed in OECD attendance and support, and the capacity of the Secretary-General to ensure a continuing recognition of the Organisation's efforts.

The OECD has now contributed widely to all of the G20 Summits since Pittsburgh, including their preparation, discussions and follow-up work to ensure the implementation of their agreements. Co-operation with the G20 was led by the Secretary-General and his Chief of Staff who led the Sherpa Unit, the attendance of the Chief Economist at G20 Finance Deputies meetings, and the work increasingly undertaken in nearly all of the OECD's Directorates to provide evidence-based data and analytical reports and proposals on a range of policy areas. This was clear evidence that the Secretary-General had achieved his early vision of the OECD as a very relevant, hub of globalisation, fulfilling in all but name the role of a secretariat for the G20.

Developing a Modified Vision: 2007–2011

The GFC had an immediate and lasting impact at the OECD, which was very conscious of its failure along with other international organisations, to forecast the crisis, as this could damage the reputation of the OECD. It had not, for example, recognised the need for monetary tightening in a timely fashion and, while some concerns had been expressed before the GFC, no clear warnings had been given, especially as to the weak capital base and lack of resilience of banking systems, notably in the USA, the UK and Europe.

As Gurría indicated, the Organisation needed to do some 'hard thinking', since dangers had been ignored and excessive deregulation and poor supervision had worsened the fragility of the financial system. Further, he stressed that what was needed was a change of mind and a change of culture to adapt to the new global, economic reality. Much of the initial rethinking, spurred on by the urgency of the situation, was summarised in 2009 in the 'OECD Strategic Response to the Financial and Economic Crisis', coordinated by Deputy Secretary General, Pier Carlo Padoan, which focused on shorter term responses to the crisis, with little fundamental questioning of existing economic and financial systems. It was also rethinking that was somewhat compartmentalised, lacking a detailed, focused narrative to pull it together and form the foundation for applicable policy options on the basis of a detailed questioning of existing systems and existing economic theory and models. In retrospect, this is not surprising, for it took some years before a comprehensive understanding of what caused the GFC was achieved.

The Strategy had two main emphases, the first on outlining policies regarding the improvement of financial systems, competition and corporate governance, with a pledge to work on strengthening and implementing principles and guidelines in these areas, areas traditionally focused upon in OECD work. The second emphasis was on measures for the restoration of long-term growth. Growth, it was argued, should be accompanied by 'low-carbon paths to growth, on eco-innovation, and on knowledge creation, all within a more equitable society that spreads opportunity and extends protection to the most vulnerable'. This emphasis led to the OECD's 'Inclusive Growth' project (dealt with at more length in Chapter 8), and to the 2018 OECD report for the MCM 'Opportunities for All: OECD Framework for Policy Action on Inclusive Growth'. It was also an emphasis dear to the heart of the Secretary-General and of his Chief of Staff, Gabriela Ramos, who supervised the project.

The development of the immediate response was followed by a period of more fundamental questioning of the OECD's role and objectives, with its past and still dominant focus on economic growth, with little consideration of the ultimate purpose of that growth. It was not that the OECD's Convention neglected that ultimate purpose, as its second paragraph noted that economic strength was essential for general well-being. Indeed, the realisation of this aim of the Convention stimulated the development of a new label to describe the revised and reframed mission of the OECD, worked out in discussions between Anthony Gooch, the Director of Public Affairs and Communications and the Secretary-General, a mission that aimed at 'Better Policies for Better Lives', shifting from the more limited, traditional OECD mission of promoting growth as an end in itself to a focus on inclusive growth as a means to well-being. This initiative was strongly supported by the Chief Statistician, Martine Durand, who supervised the development of the 'Better Life Initiative', focused on promoting a multi-dimensional measurement of well-being to enhance the frequently used, but narrow measure of GDP.

The newly-developed vision emerged in 2011 in the form of the Fiftieth Anniversary Vision Statement from Council, a vision that guided many developments at the OECD in the next 10 years. In the Statement, the Members recommitted themselves to the essential mission of promoting stronger, but now cleaner, fairer economic growth, and to raise employment and living standards by designing policies to improve the well-being of the peoples of the world. Such policies built, at least in part, upon new approaches and lessons learnt from the GFC. They resolved also to make the OECD a more effective and inclusive global policy network, encouraging even greater participation by other countries in its work, to reduce inequality and to support inclusive growth.

The elements of the vision were not entirely new but they were given a new emphasis by Council, based in large part on the ideas that had been increasingly developed since the GFC by the Secretary-General and his staff. The main ideas were: to achieve cleaner, fairer more inclusive economic growth, with an emphasis on the more equitable distribution of the benefits of globalisation, and improving the well-being of all people. And to make the OECD a global policy network, with an increased emphasis on the participation of non-member, mindful that adherence and commitment to the OECD's policies and standards would be more likely and more enduring if non-member countries were also fully involved in their development. This did not mean that there would be any dramatic increase in OECD membership, rather an increasingly global adoption of its policies and standards and a step beyond the earlier vision of the OECD as a hub of globalisation.

The 50th anniversary of the OECD in 2011 also saw the renewal of the Secretary-General's tenure for a further five years. In a speech to the OECD Ambassadors celebrating its renewal, Gurría stressed that the goal of ensuring the relevance of the OECD was still at the forefront of his efforts, but that now there needed to be a new emphasis on more inclusive and green growth, supported by a two-pronged strategy that moved beyond assisting Members in designing policies to include policy options for effective implementation. This involved working closely with Members – the essence of what he described as 'Going National', outlined in Chapter 6. The second part of the strategy was to increase the OECD's role as a global standard setter. This role required the Organisation to work closely with Members and, he stressed, major emerging economies. The basic elements of the strategy, with its emphasis on inclusive growth, were endorsed at the 2012 MCM, although with a greater stress on the need for continuing structural reforms in Member countries, compared to the emphasis in Gurría's 2011 mandate renewal speech.

It was clear that the vision and Gurría's interpretation of it would need 'fleshing out' in more detail, assisted by a continuing and more fundamental rethinking. As a result, Gurría agreed to a more centralised focus, in the shape of a small unit in his Office, the New Approaches to Economic Challenges (NAEC) Initiative (described at more length in Chapter 11), led by his Chief of Staff. It was by no means an easy task to persuade Council of the value of NAEC, with several Members opposing its development. However, lobbying in national capitals, together with the support of some Ambassadors, achieved the necessary agreement. The aims of NAEC were: to supervise 26 individual projects taking place across the OECD, focused on developing a better understanding of the causes of the GFC; and on the basis of that understanding, to establish a framework for better policy advice that could be incorporated in what came to be described as the 'Strategic OECD Policy Agenda for Inclusive Growth'. As the Secretary-General noted, the problem was that the traditional models did not reflect the reality of the economy or of people's lives in that economy; and they did not anticipate how the pain of the recession would lead to social and political crises.

Cleaner, Fairer More Inclusive Growth in a Global Policy Network: 2011–2016

As described in Chapter 8, work on the Inclusive Growth project developed rapidly in 2011–2016, strongly supported by the Secretary-General and his then Chief of Staff, Gabriela Ramos, including a new 'dashboard' of indicators on issues such as income, growth, employment, education, environment and governance, to assist countries and their people monitor progress toward inclusive growth goals. In 2018, the OECD launched a report for the MCM, *Opportunities for All: OECD Framework for Policy Action on Inclusive Growth*. It showed that countries' efforts to remedy inequalities were variable in their impact, with signs of progress, but that greater effort was needed because opportunities were worsening for low-income groups. The report therefore called for an 'urgent and concerted effort' on the part of governments to drive more inclusive, sustainable economic growth that would benefit all in society.

The first phase of the NAEC initiative also generally progressed well in this period, with its findings and recommendations regarding the causes of the GFC being contained in its 2015 report 'Final NAEC Synthesis: New Approaches to Economic Challenges'. The report contained a wide range of proposed changes in approach and method at the OECD, with the Chief of Staff stressing the need to achieve a better balance between efficiency, equity and sustainability, a view vigorously supported by Gurría. The changes were endorsed by Council, following which they began to be implemented, though at varying rates.

The 50th anniversary goal of the OECD as the centre of a more effective and inclusive global policy network was developed in more detail over the next two years, leading to Council's 2013 agreement to open accession discussions with two Latin American countries, Colombia and Costa Rica, and two more European countries, Latvia, and Lithuania, their selection representing a balance between competing preferences among Council members. Council also reiterated its earlier desire for the accession of the Russian Federation and the continuation of work to this end, which came to an end with the Russian annexation of Crimea in 2014.

Council also agreed to increase cooperation with what are now known as the OECD's Key Partners, Brazil, China, India, Indonesia and South Africa, in all aspects of the OECD's work. The Secretary-General was invited to speedily implement the OECD Southeast Asia Regional Programme and to renew efforts to integrate countries from the region in the Organisation's work, including through possible accession. He was also asked to explore and develop recommendations to Council on how to further strengthen the regional component of the OECD's global relations, with a focus on Africa and Latin America, as well as the Middle East and North Africa (MENA). Finally, it was agreed to continue to deepen the OECD's relationships with, in particular, the G20 and G7, but also APEC and ASEAN.

As described in Chapter 10 on Tax, one of the most significant steps in developing the goal of a global policy network was the Base Erosion and Profit Shifting (BEPS) project and its support from the G20, which asked the OECD in 2012 to develop a BEPS Action Plan, approved at the 2013 G20 meeting. An OECD BEPS Multilateral Instrument (MLI), was adopted by the G20 on 24 November 2016 and has now been adopted by over 135 countries. The increasingly global work on tax was accompanied by the growing globalisation of the OECD's work within the Policy Framework for Investment, first published in 2006, but significantly updated in 2016 with a far more extensive participation by non-OECD members, an impetus continued with the biannual, Freedom of Investment Roundtables.

In addition, a number of the OECD's legal instruments, standards and norms became increasingly global in their membership, notably the Convention on Combating Bribery of Foreign Public Officials in International Business Transactions, the Declaration on Automatic Exchange of Information for Tax Purposes, the Declaration on International Investment and Multinational Enterprises, the G20/OECD Principles of Corporate Governance, and the OECD Guidelines for Multinational Enterprises. The opening up to adherence by non-members of the Code of Liberalisation of Capital Movements was particularly important, as the G20 was also focusing on coordinating capital movements and the Codes were initially not seen as a useful tool in that regard, given their previously restricted membership. The close relationship maintained with the G20 by the Secretary-General, his Sherpa and senior OECD officials was increasingly important as a conduit for their global dissemination.

Latvia gained OECD membership in 2016, Lithuania in 2018, Colombia in 2020, and Costa Rica joined in 2021. Council discussions, about enlargement of six prospective members (Argentina, Brazil, Bulgaria, Croatia, Peru and Romania) which started before 2017, have failed so far to reach consensus.

Consolidating and Increasing Achievements, But Also Increasing Pessimism: 2016–2021

Gurría's plans for 2016–2021 were outlined in 2015 in two documents prepared to support his third and final term in office, 'Transforming the OECD Impact, Inclusiveness and Relevance', which listed his claimed achievements, and '21 for 21: A Proposal for Consolidation and Further Transformation of the OECD'. The latter proposals were aimed at informing a dialogue with Members, leading, he hoped, to a jointly defined roadmap to consolidate the OECD's transformation by 2021. In it he listed eight overarching goals to focus efforts:

1. Making our Organisation even more useful and relevant to its Members and partner countries.
2. Redefining the growth narrative to put the well-being of people at the centre of our efforts.
3. Identifying emerging policy challenges, while reinforcing our capacity to understand and address them.
4. Supporting the global agenda and collective policy action.
5. Developing further our productivity and competitiveness agenda by leveraging our multidisciplinary knowledge.
6. Strengthening and maximising the impact of our existing standards, as well as identifying the areas in which we need to develop new ones.
7. Continuing to enhance the global character of our Organisation.
8. Ensuring effective and efficient financial, administrative, communications and management practices within the Organisation.

The list contains no new specific, major goals, in contrast to those he had when taking office in 2006, such as those related to water, migration and health, and as revised following the GFC. Rather, in line with the '21 for 21' document's title, the listed goals were aimed at increasing the performance of the OECD along a number of existing dimensions, in effect to consolidate and to improve on what was already in train, not to enter significant new ground.

The goals in '21 for 21', helped secure the Secretary-General's third term in office and provided a general framework in which almost any policy aim endorsed by the 2015 and 2016 MCMs could be incorporated. This proved to be the case for the 2015 MCM, which applauded the OECD's achievements and urged further or accelerated work in a number of areas, rather than dramatic or major new areas of work. '21 for 21' also provided the framework for Gurría's 'Strategic Orientations' for 2016 and the longer term, in which his emphasis was on harvesting the results from 'Initiatives, workstreams and strategies that are in the process of maturing and bearing fruit'.

Gurría's aims in 2017 were clearly based on those in '21 for 21', but now noted an urgent need to speed up the transformation of policy responses to keep pace with the pressures of a rapidly changing world. This could include, he noted, the exploration of the value of the creation of ad hoc 'crack teams' of experts from across different OECD Directorates that could be rapidly deployed to support countries when needed, a possible new dimension of his ongoing, 'Go National', drive.

While not new, he also indicated the need for Members to enable him to 're-spond promptly', to the formal requests for membership received from Argentina, Bulgaria, Croatia, Kazakhstan, Malta, Peru, Romania and Sri Lanka, and to consider other expressions of interest. This plea was to no avail, as three years later little or no progress had been made in these directions. As the Secretary-General noted in his 2020 Strategic Orientations, discussions on a new enlargement round had been 'prolonged and contentious', with Members seemingly impervious to his arguments for enlargement, despite the progress that had been made, for example, by Argentina, Brazil and Romania in aligning themselves with OECD policies, standards and agreements.

As the following chapters in this book illustrate, significant new and accelerated developments continued to characterise the work of the OECD in 2016–2021, such as the documentation of climate finance for the UNFCCC and the use by the WTO of OECD indicators helping it to achieve the Bali Agreement on Trade Facilitation, work strongly supported by Gurría and much appreciated by his counterparts. It was also a period that saw the launch of the Centre on Well-Being, Inclusiveness, Sustainability and Equality Opportunity (WISE), the development of the OECD Principles on Artificial Intelligence, and work with the European Commission's DG Reform as part of the Going National agenda, examined in the following chapters.

However, while much of the OECD's work was going well, the issue of multilateralism began to come to the fore. In Gurría's 2017 Strategic Orientations paper, for example, he stressed the importance of strengthening multilateral co-operation. In his view, societies in OECD countries seemed increasingly sceptical about the process of globalisation and the architecture and values of multilateral co-operation and openness, with the emergence of new forms of nationalism, isolationism, populism and protectionism. It was a theme reiterated with increased urgency in his 2018 Strategic Orientations, where he argued that multilateralism was at a crossroads, and its ability to provide solutions to global challenges was increasingly being put to the test, with some governments preferring to advance their goals by national or ad hoc responses, rather than through multilateral ones.

The urgency of the Secretary-General's calls for strengthened multilateralism, also expressed in speeches to a variety of audiences, did not, however, meet with very strong support from the 2018 MCM, though it did note that enhanced international co-operation and better implementation of international agreements by all countries would help to ensure that globalisation worked for everyone and that in this regard, it highly valued the OECD's continued contribution. It would have been difficult for the MCM to have agreed otherwise, given the clear opposition to at least some aspects of multilateralism of two of its leading Members, as evident in the UK's decision to withdraw from membership of the EU, and President Trump's minimal regard for several international organisations, including his failure to appoint a person of ambassadorial status to the OECD.

Nevertheless, in the context of the outbreak of the COVID-19 pandemic, in his 2020 Strategic Orientations, the Secretary-General persisted in his view that multilateralism was under threat, pointing out that the deteriorating geopolitical situation had paralysed key OECD dossiers, including enlargement, for more than three years – in the latter case a similar situation to that he had faced on taking office in 2006. It had also affected, he argued, the OECD's global relations strategy, including its engagement with Key Partners, whose alignment to OECD's work, standards and values was critical to help level the global playing field and maintain the OECD's relevance and impact.

The pessimism evident in the Secretary-General's views regarding multilateralism was even more apparent in his 2020 call for strong support from the OECD's Members if the Organisation was to fulfil its mandates in the years after the end of the pandemic. He noted that it had become more time consuming and more complex to gain agreement in Council, with a resulting failure to reach consensus on issues of strategic importance to the OECD agenda, including the issuing of agreed Ministerial Council Statements at the annual MCM, enlargement to new Members, adequate budgets, resourcing, and funding of pensions, among other important issues.

The result was that, he asserted, the OECD was finding it harder to operate, harder to advance, harder to focus on substantive agendas, while the trust and the convergence of views of its Members had declined, making consensus increasingly difficult. These were strong views, that could, perhaps, only be put forward with credibility by a Secretary-General in the final months of a 15-year term in Office that had commenced with his passion, commitment and a range of successful reforms in an increasingly transformed Organisation, but an Organisation now threatened by the lack of cohesion of its Members.

Conclusion

Secretary-General Gurría's leadership has experienced a number of phases during his 15-year period in office. The first was a settling-in period in 2006–2007, marked by his leading an initially cautious, but rapidly widening set of reforms as he became more acquainted with the Organisation, its strengths and weaknesses. His desire for reform became evident in the shape of his reallocation of resources to boost work on health, migration and water; the reshaping and rapid development of a new global relations strategy for the OECD, especially in relation to the G8 and the G20; financial reforms; and a Council agreement on enlargement. These were exciting developments, stimulating staff to greater efforts and achievements, and accompanied by a necessary growth and centralisation of authority at the OECD to provide the increased capacity necessary for such work, especially in the Office of the Secretary-General and the Global Relations Secretariat.

The period from mid-2007 to 2011, with the onset of the GFC, was the first major challenge of Gurría's leadership capacity, as the OECD faced the greatest test of its existence, one in which its most basic assumptions and methods were called into question, both internally and externally. He proved well capable of meeting the challenge as he and his senior staff not only commenced and completed a detailed assessment of the OECD's work, its strengths and weaknesses, but took the opportunity offered by the G20 to increasingly extend the reach and influence of its existing instruments, standards and norms, and to develop modified and new policies that gained greater, global acceptance, for example, in relation to climate change (as examined in Chapter 7). It also saw, in 2011, the launch of the 'Better Policies for Better Lives' emphasis in OECD work.

The period from approximately 2011 to 2016 and the commencement of his second term in office was, as one of his senior officials put it, perhaps a 'golden age', for the Secretary-General. It saw the full flowering of work on tax, inclusive growth, and other policy areas; successful moves to further enlargement of membership; and the extension of the role and status of the OECD in an increasingly global policy network.

The next and final period, from 2016 to 2021, became one of increasing challenges for the Secretary-General as he tried to help the OECD and its Members benefit from the many reforms and changes that had occurred under his leadership in the previous 10 years. The challenges came largely from two sources, one internal, the other external. The first was the frustrating and worrying difficulties he faced in gaining Council support for, in particular, an expansion of budgetary resources and a further extension of OECD membership. His by now well-honed leadership skills and experience were stretched to the limit in both these areas, as Council kept a very tight constraint on budgets, and could come to no agreement as to the selection of candidates for further enlargement.

The second challenge was the working environment for multilateralism and the dramatic impact of the COVID pandemic in 2020–2021 on the OECD's staff and operations. In contrast to his frustrating relations with Council, the latter was an area in which his leadership skills came to the fore, strongly supported by the staff of the OECD as a whole, in developing 'virtual' work systems that enabled the continuation of much of their operations in most difficult circumstances and supporting Members in their crisis response.

As 2020 came to an end and 2021 commenced, a number of changes saw a lessening of tension in relations with Council. The first was an agreement for a joint statement by Members at the October 2020 MCM, after a four-year gap without one. The second was Council's agreement in December 2020 to a PWB for 2021–2022 that retained ZRG as its basis, as proposed by the Secretary-General. The third was the establishment of the Biden Administration in 2021, replacing the Trump Administration, including the probable appointment of a US Ambassador to the OECD for the first time in four years. It must have been with a deep sense of relief that Secretary-General Gurría saw the Biden Administration replace that of Trump in 2021, with the prospect this brought for the rebuilding of trust among OECD members, a heightening of consensus and progress on key items on Council's agenda.

It is to the Secretary-General's credit that, while he faced increasing difficulties in Council, the OECD continued to produce, as described in the other chapters of this book, a range of significant new developments, as regards both its internal management and its policy outputs, such as the launch of the International Programme for Climate Action (IPAC) near the end of his mandate.

5 Going National

The OECD Convention stipulates that the aim of the Organisation is – in a nutshell – to achieve for its Members the highest sustainable economic growth, employment and standard of living, while maintaining financial stability. In other words, to develop policies and standards that will assist Members' economic growth, both domestically and internationally. This has involved not only relevant, evidence-based research and policy developments, but also reviews and assessments of Members' policies in relation to economic growth, often by means of peer review. Over time, this has gradually widened in scope to include almost all of the OECD Members' policy areas, including education, social policy, the environment, health, and governance as Members have come to realise their importance for economic growth.

Much of the analytical work done by the OECD until the 2000s focused on reviewing existing policies, designing possible new policies, and developing standards, with less emphasis on how to implement policy change and reform, and tailor it to the specific Members' needs. As a result, there had been a growing number of requests from Members for more specific and tailored guidance. Further, Ministers encouraged the OECD during the 2006, 2007 and 2008 Ministerial Council Meetings to intensify its work on the political economy of reform and increase its support to governments in their reform efforts, notably as regards structural reform, especially in the aftermath of the global financial crisis.

The OECD responded by intensifying work on two existing, linked projects. The first was the 'Political Economy of Reform', commenced in 2007 to identify and better understand the factors behind successful reforms and to provide direct support to Member countries in their domestic reform efforts. The second was 'Making Reform Happen', that commenced in 2007, led by Deputy Secretary-General Aart de Geus, that built on the work undertaken in the first project and focused on the stages beyond policy design to explore and help Member countries introduce reforms effectively. Both projects were strongly endorsed by Secretary-General Gurría, and Committees were encouraged to incorporate work on the implementation of reforms in their projects.

One of the outcomes, for example, of the development and production of the 2010 Innovation Strategy, was a call for the development of an innovation policy 'handbook' to provide more specific and tailored guidance to policymakers seeking to improve their countries' innovation performance. A similar call had been made for a toolkit to accompany the Green Growth Strategy and, in part, had been stimulated by other OECD toolkits, for example, the Policy Framework for Investment toolkit.

In 2011, the OECD's Fiftieth Anniversary Vision Statement stressed the need to make the Organisation a more effective and inclusive global policy network whose essential mission was to promote stronger, cleaner, fairer economic growth and to

https://doi.org/10.1515/9783110735833-005

raise employment and living standards. A more effective OECD was a theme picked up in Secretary-General Gurría's 'Strategic Orientations' for 2013, where he stressed the need to increase the OECD's impact on national agendas by 'Going National', working hand-in-hand with governments to create policy solutions tailored to their challenges, as was the case with the OECD's Skills Strategy. In particular, he noted, the Organisation should further focus work on the implementation side of the policy cycle by providing officials with capacity-building programmes, workshops and training.

From one perspective, this new emphasis on impact, relevance, tailored advice and 'Going National', can be viewed simply as a continuation of the implementation-focused Political Economy of Reform and Making Reform Happen projects. It can also be seen as a marketing strategy, drawing attention to the support given to Members' national policies, and therefore very much a 'reminder' of the OECD's value. However, 'Going National' was not a specific programme or project, or a marketing ploy, but a message to all OECD officials that the Secretary-General expected a more effective impact on national policies by the Organisation, one in which implementation should gain greater attention. Going national was emphasized again in the Secretary-General's Strategic Orientations in 2014 and at the closing press conference following the 2014 Ministerial Council Meeting. Specifically, he extended 'Going National' with the launch of country programmes in Kazakhstan, Morocco, Peru and Thailand, while continuing to work closely with Ukraine.

The message of 'Going National' was also linked to the OECD's 'Inclusive Growth', initiative in 2015, as well as the structural reform efforts of Members, by stressing that such developments could be assisted by providing them with country-specific advice and recommendations that take into account policy trade-offs and complementarities. Further, as part of these efforts, the OECD provided increased support in the shape of the 'Better Policies' series and 'Getting It Right' studies, country policy briefs led by the Office of the Secretary-General. These outputs complemented the Economic Surveys and country-specific thematic policy reviews, leveraging the OECD's multi-disciplinarity expertise to provide more comprehensive advice. The 'Better Policies Series' drew upon the OECD's comparative work to identify what were considered to be best practice policies and standards, tailored to meet the specific priorities of governments in their reform efforts.

The 'Going National' message and its importance was also noted in the Secretary-General's 2016 re-election bid, and specifically in his '21 for 21: A proposal for consolidation and further transformation of the OECD'. 'Going national' also featured in the Secretary-General's 2019 and 2020 Strategic Orientations. In the latter, it was presented as one of 10 actions that would 'anchor' the OECD's future work. The OECD would strengthen its internal coordination and communication in order to help ensure effective, national-level advice and assistance.

The following sections focus on a range of examples of work at least partly inspired by the 'Going National' emphasis, which demonstrate the increased extent to which OECD policy advice has been tailored to Members' individual circumstances.

Going National in Practice

In 1994 the OECD published its influential Jobs Strategy, emphasising the role of flexible labour and product markets for tackling high and persistent unemployment. In 2006, a Reassessed Jobs Strategy was published, placing greater emphasis on promoting labour force participation and improving job quality. In 2016, the OECD Ministers of Employment and Labour gave a mandate to the OECD to review and update the Jobs Strategy in light of the profound labour market transformations following the digital revolution, globalisation and demographic changes. A new OECD Jobs Strategy was launched in 2018. It provides detailed policy recommendations across a broad range of policy areas in order to help countries address these challenges. It goes beyond job quantity and considers job quality and inclusiveness as central policy priorities, while emphasising the importance of resilience and adaptability for good economic and labour market performance in a changing world of work.

In 2019, the new Jobs Strategy was complemented by a publication, 'Going National: Implementing the OECD Jobs Strategy', that, in line with the 'Going National' emphasis, focused on the national level implementation of the Jobs Strategy. It did so by identifying countries' main policy challenges and developing a range of broad policy options to address them, stressing the importance of a country's initial conditions, such as the state of the business cycle, its fiscal and administrative capacity, past reforms, preferences, and demography. In other words, it provided the means to tailor the more general Jobs Strategy advice to a country's specific circumstances, using, for example, the online 'dashboard' of the new Jobs Strategy and the elements of broad policy packages to deal with the issues. These, in turn, can provide the basis for developing detailed, country-specific reform strategies. One such example is the Action Plan for Youth which focuses on providing advice on specific youth policies, tackling the youth unemployment crisis, and strengthening the long-term employment prospects for youth.

The emphasis on Going National can also be seen in the Tax Inspectors Without Borders (TIWB) joint OECD/UNDP initiative launched in July 2015 to strengthen developing countries' national auditing capacity and multinationals' compliance worldwide. This initiative has gained increased relevance in as a practical tool to help developing countries collect all the taxes due from multinational enterprises. According to the latest annual report, up to the end of 2020, TIWB assistance had delivered USD 775 million in additional revenue recovered from an overall tax assessment of over USD 2.37 billion.

Similarly, the Partnership in Statistics for Development in the 21st Century (PARIS21) focuses on encouraging a better use of statistics in developing countries by providing support and strengthening their National Statistical Systems. PARIS21 was founded in November 1999 by the UN, the European Commission, the OECD, the IMF, and the World Bank. Today, it works with over 90 countries, and focuses on five key impact areas: advocating and funding statistics; building and sharing knowledge; developing innovative solutions for statistics; engaging in international initiatives; and strengthening statistical systems.

In its efforts to further promote its work on going national, the OECD created the Centre for Entrepreneurship, SMEs, Regions and Cities in 2017. The Centre's work to-date has focused on inter-dependencies between people, places and firms in policy-making. The Centre has been attempting to increase policy effectiveness and helping countries 'go national' as well as 'go local' through its role in connecting key stakeholder, national and sub-national governments, local actors and firms.

The OECD has also supported Mexican governments with an ambitious reform package over the last 15 years. The package provided support for the design, promotion and implementation of structural reforms on labour, fiscal, finance, competition, telecoms, anti-corruption, education, skills, and gender equality. It also provided support for the development and implementation of policies and frameworks on open government data, digitalisation, the effectiveness of social policies and poverty reduction policies, health (obesity), housing, pensions, sectoral competition, disaster risk, water management, environment, tourism, and cities and urban development. It also helped launch a multi-state programme to help schools combat gender stereotypes and promote the interest of children and young girls in STEM subjects and careers. The OECD has also worked with 19 Mexican state governments, supporting them on a range of key policy areas, such as regulatory improvement, competitiveness, integrity, public procurement, regional development and skills.

The OECD also supported Mexico in the design, creation and operation of autonomous bodies on education, competition, telecommunications, energy, and access to public information, with significant impact. For example, the Telecommunication and Broadcasting Reviews resulted in a significant increase in the number of subscriptions to mobile broad band services (50 million extra subscriptions) and a significant drop of prices of mobile telecommunications between 2012 and 2017.

Work with national administrations has continued during the COVID-19 crisis, for example with Colombia, where the OECD has been working with the authorities to support an inclusive, resilient and sustainable recovery. This collaboration builds on the roadmap launched by the Colombian Government in 2020 ('New Commitment for the Future of Colombia') which aims to address the socio-economic challenges generated by the COVID-19 pandemic by bringing together different stakeholders around an overarching national agreement to promote the economic reactivation of Colombia. The OECD will focus on supporting Colombia's efforts to develop and implement integrated policy solutions to achieve such a recovery, notably as regards social protection and tackling labour market informality; competition and regulation; and enhancing productivity and sustainability.

The OECD has also provided advice to the reform efforts of non-member countries. The signature of a two-year Country Programme Agreement between the OECD and Kazakhstan, for example, led to an important volume of work focused on supporting reform efforts across a wide range of policy domains and has provided an opportunity for Kazakhstan to increase its participation in a number of OECD Committees and their subsidiary bodies. As a result, Kazakhstan has also adhered to a growing number of OECD instruments under the Programme. A new agreement, which runs until end of 2022, provides a framework for further co-operation and reflects the commitment of both the OECD and Kazakhstan to build on the success of the Country Programme.

The OECD's Support for Reform in EU Member Countries and the EU's Structural Reform Programme

The OECD has a complex relationship with the EU dating back to 1961 when the EU was granted full access to the OECD's deliberations – more than mere Participant status. This has allowed EU representatives to participate and speak in any OECD meeting (apart from meetings involving internal organisation) without being invited, though without voting rights when legal acts are adopted by the Council (apart from the Development Assistance Committee (DAC) and the Development Centre, where the EU is a full member). Given that the OECD works in nearly all of the policy areas covered by the EU and its related agencies, a continuing and close cooperation provides benefits for both organisations.

Today, 22 EU Members are also Members of the OECD. Although the EU does not contribute to Part I of the OECD budget, through voluntary contributions (VCs) it provides approximately a quarter of all voluntary funding. The growth in VCs from the EU over the last decade has underpinned the strengthened partnership. In addition, the EU Member states provide approximately 40% of the assessed, Part I budget contributions. In other words, while not a Member, the EU is a significant player at the OECD.

EU representatives routinely chair, co-chair or vice-chair substantive OECD Committees, and are members of over 200 of those Committees and working parties. Hence, when examining the relationship between the EU and the OECD, one is in fact referring to a large and varying set of relationships. One of the most recent of these relationships began in 2015, through a close collaboration between the OECD (led by the Office of the Secretary-General), the Government of Greece under Prime Minister Alexis Tsipras, and the European Commission. It was based on an agreement signed in March 2015 between the OECD and Greece for the development of a range of projects. The agreement created a Joint Steering Committee (informally known as 'the

Taskforce') which was Chaired by the Chief of Staff, Gabriela Ramos, from the OECD and the Alternate Minister for International Economic Relations, and later Finance Minister, Mr Euclid Tsakalotos, from Greece.

The role of the Committee was twofold. First, to take an active part in the negotiation of projects with the European Commission and ensure that the needs of all parties were met and the project contracts were signed. Second, to provide advice and support to OECD experts assigned to the projects, and also to the Greek authorities. The first three projects were a Competition Assessment Review (2016); followed by an Education Policy Review (2016–2018); and a project to provide technical support on anti-corruption to the Greek authorities (2016–2017). It was estimated that the Competition Assessment Review of Greece, with its recommended reforms of regulations in the sectors of e-commerce, wholesale trade, construction services, media, pharmaceuticals and chemicals, would have a positive impact on the Greek economy of around €414 million. In March 2018, the European Commission's compliance report found that the Greek authorities had implemented all recommendations.

The OECD-European Commission collaboration became more structured in 2019 when an overall agreement was signed for the implementation of an additional 38 reform projects in 18 EU member states, with the OECD providing staff expertise in a range of policy areas from a number of its Directorates, coordinated by staff in the Office of the Secretary-General. In 2020, the collaboration with DG REFORM grew to include 47 additional reform implementation projects in 22 EU countries, amounting to a total of 85 projects. The collaboration has helped produce important reforms, for example, improved labour market integration in Slovenia; stronger public procurement systems in Greece; environmental fiscal reform in Italy; and improved housing affordability in the Czech Republic.

As a result of the adverse impact of the COVID-19 pandemic, the EU established the Technical Support Instrument (TSI) in 2021. DG REFORM has been provided with a substantially increased budget of €864 million for the period 2021–2027. In addition to assisting national authorities to design, develop and implement reforms, the TSI also aims to support EU Member States as they prepare, amend, implement and revise their national recovery and resilience plans. The OECD continues to collaborate closely with DG REFORM in the framework of the new TSI and will implement 67 TSI projects in 2021.

Conclusion

It was very much the drive of the OECD's leadership under Secretary-General Angel Gurría that led to the development of the OECD's Going National emphasis and the provision of support for both Members and non-members. Going National was one of many conscious decisions by the Secretary-General to transform the OECD into a 'do-tank', not only a 'think tank', by providing targeted policy advice with a focus on implementation.

In this respect, 'Going National', was not a programme or project, per se, but a repeated message to officials and Members that emphasised the need to maintain and, where possible, to increase the quality and relevance of the OECD's policy advice, responding to Members' needs. It drew attention to the need to utilise the multi-disciplinary strengths of the OECD and the need to include a strong focus on tailored, country-specific implementation advice to deliver on reforms. Those strengths were demonstrated by their use in the EU's Structural Reform Research Projects in 2019–2020 and the continuing demand from DG REFORM and EU countries for OECD services.

6 Going Global

'Going global', a term used frequently by the OECD in its publications and by its officials over the last decade and more, reflects the desire of the Council and, in particular, the Secretary-General, to expand the breadth of the Organisation's activities, its legal instruments and influence outside its Members. The focus was to be upon what became known as its Key Partners and a growing range of selected regions and related regional and global organisations, but also countries interested in aligning themselves with the Organisation. Going global was a policy that came to permeate most, if not all of the work and activities of the OECD during Secretary-General Gurría's long tenure, bringing with it a rapid increase in staff, largely centralised in what became the Global Relations Secretariat, and a greatly increased focus on global relations by the External Relations Committee and the substantive Committees and their associated Directorates and Centres.

The increase in OECD membership in the last two decades reflected this same basic desire, but more selective and narrower, undertaken on a very cautious basis, following lengthy periods of often contentious discussion between Members, much to the frustration of Gurría and his senior officials. A larger, but still restricted membership, was seen as a way of making the Organisation's standards and policies gain global influence without it becoming an organisation with universal membership. This was to be done by recruiting to its ranks only those countries that were like-minded in their values and significant players in the global economy, bringing a degree of global diversity to the Organisation's membership. These basic criteria were, however, applied in a very flexible fashion to include countries such as Costa Rica, with a population of only five million and by no means a 'significant player' in the global economy.

The Emergence of the OECD Global Relations Strategy (GRS): 2001–2005

As indicated in Chapter 3, the OECD's external relations have been many and complex, but until the 1990s they had a relatively low profile, both within and outside the Organisation, only occasionally attracting sustained attention in Council and senior levels of the Secretariat, with the exception of its Development Cooperation Directorate and Development Centre. This situation changed in the 1990s with the rise of the 'Asian Tigers' (Hong Kong (China), Singapore, South Korea and Chinese Taipei), the breakup of the Soviet Union and the rising interest of newly-independent, ex-Soviet states, eastern European states, then the Russian Federation, in membership of the OECD. The OECD's first major programme of work with non-Members

https://doi.org/10.1515/9783110735833-006

was almost entirely focused on the former centrally-planned economies in Europe and Asia, with four of them (Czech Republic, Hungary, Poland, Slovak Republic) gaining OECD membership by 2000.

The growing external activities were supervised from 1998 by a new Centre for Co-operation with Non-Members (CCNM), a unit within the OECD's General Secretariat, although most of the implementation was undertaken by one or more of the OECD's specialised policy Directorates. The CCNM advised the Secretary-General on policy and developments with non-Members and provided the principal contact point for non-Members. It also provided assistance to OECD Members in developing the strategic orientations and main priorities for the OECD's 'outreach' to non-members.

The CCNM was guided in its work by the Council's Committee on Co-operation with non-members (CCN), later replaced by the External Relations Committee, and was part of the OECD's 'Development Cluster', together with the Development Co-operation Directorate (DCD), the Development Centre and the Sahel and West-Africa Club (SWAC). The number of observerships in OECD Committees grew from 57 in 1998 to 95 in 2003, involving more than 20 countries and over 30 Committees. By 2000 there were nine separate programmes of work, consisting of three multi-country, thematic programmes and six Country and Regional Programmes. In 2002, OECD and New Partnership for Africa's Development (NEPAD) ministers agreed to conduct further dialogue to consider the scope for OECD-NEPAD co-operation, building on existing OECD programmes.

It became clear that this proliferation of new activities required a comprehensive strategy to coordinate and maximise their impact and, in 2001, Secretary-General Johnston asked the Ambassadors to examine the OECD's role and, in particular, what should be the future membership of the OECD (16 countries were then enquiring about possible membership) and its relations with non-Member countries. A proposed new Strategy for Enlargement and Outreach resulted (the Noboru Report, 2004), and was adopted by the MCM in 2005, becoming the foundation on which the OECD's global relations strategy developed in the years ahead. Importantly, for the first time in the OECD's history, a systematic accession process was also agreed for potential Members, with three key criteria for determining the eligibility of candidate countries: like-mindedness, significant player in the global economy and a degree of global diversity within the Organisation's membership.

The Strategy, adopted in 2005, was a broad one, enabling a considerable degree of flexibility in the content and direction of work programmes, with the Organisation's global relations aims being:
– Contributing to the harmonious functioning of the global economy
– Promoting shared prosperity
– Encouraging shared knowledge for better public policy

The bulk of global activities, as previously was the case, were embedded in the various Programme of Work and Budget (PWB) Output Groups and continued to be undertaken by the Directorates. In addition, Output Group 5.2 Global Relations was the responsibility of the CCNM, advising the Secretary-General on general policy and developments in relations with non-Members and providing strategic guidance to the Directorates.

The new strategy was focused more sharply on three main approaches to the OECD's global relations: regional approaches, country programmes, and global forums with, in addition, the direct involvement of 21 non-Members involved in the work of one or more Committees as full participants or regular observers. However, there was no decision from Council at this time as to whether or not there would be any enlargement of membership (Secretary-General Johnston noted that 'This is regrettable, and I believe that Members should redouble efforts to break the current logjam'), nor the priority to be given to the three approaches. This was to come in May 2007, following lengthy and sometimes contentious discussions led by the new Secretary-General, Angel Gurría in 2006–2007.

The Development of the Global Relations Strategy and Enlargement: 2007–2021

The 2007 MCM Resolution on Enlargement and Enhanced Engagement nominated the first set of prospective members since the Slovak Republic in 2000: Chile, Estonia, Israel, the Russian Federation and Slovenia. It also emphasised the desire for more intense engagement with five important non-Members that came to be known as the Key Partners in 2012: Brazil, the People's Republic of China, India, Indonesia and South Africa, 'with a view to their possible membership'. It was also agreed that there should be an expansion of the OECD's relations with selected countries and regions of strategic interest, giving priority to Southeast Asia, to identify countries for possible membership. Council approved a substantial budget increase of €12 million (24%), to support the new programme of enhanced engagement in the 2009–2010 biennium.

A number of Global Forums were developed on an ad hoc basic in 2000–2006 as approved by Council (2001–2002 Forums on Agriculture, Competition, Governance, International Direct Investment, the Knowledge Economy, Sustainable Development, Taxation and Trade; 2005 Education, Development). Each Forum consisted of a network of policymakers, academics, industry representatives and experts from OECD and non-OECD countries that enabled the Organisation to improve the relevance and expand the reach of its standards. Also, it was felt that they helped foster convergence of views among relevant players on policy standards and good practices, and to identify emerging issues.

The Forums were reviewed by the ERC in 2007, with its recommendation for a standardised framework for their creation and management being endorsed by Council in December 2008. A set of voluntary guidelines for their management was also issued in 2008. The ERC recommended that the substantive Committees should be given responsibility for the Global Forums, using them as their primary tool to involve stakeholders other than Members and Observers. While the ERC review felt that the aims of the Forums should remain as already agreed, it found that the title 'Global Forum' had been used for a number of 'wildcat' Global Forums other than the 10 recognised ones, which was to be avoided.

A further number of Forums have been developed over time, the most recent being the Global Forum on Digital Security for Prosperity (2018), the Global Forum on the Future of Education and Skills 2030 (2020), and the Global Forum on Nuclear Education, Science, Technology and Policy (2021). It should be noted that the Global Forum on Transparency and Exchange of Information for Tax Purposes, established in 2009, and now with 162 members, is not a Global Forum in the sense of the 2008 Framework and is organised under a different set of rules, in line with its broader functions and responsibilities.

The importance of the GRS was increased with the 2011 Fiftieth Anniversary Vision Statement, which asked that the OECD position itself as a more effective and inclusive Global Policy Network, based on high standards, with the goal of developing effective and innovative policy choices for governments around the world. This reinforced the emphasis on making OECD standards increasingly global in their reach, and was rapidly incorporated into new, revised Country and Regional Programmes, such as that for Southeast Asia, and in relations with other international organisations and groupings such as the G20.

In 2013 Council agreed to open accession discussions with Colombia, Latvia, Lithuania and Costa Rica, as well as to strengthen relations with the five Key Partners, Brazil, China, India, Indonesia and South Africa. Council also agreed to develop a range of regional programmes, especially with Southeast Asia, with a view to identifying countries for possible membership.

The importance of the GRS was further underlined in the Secretary-General's '21 for 21 Proposal for Consolidation and Further Transformation of the OECD', issued in 2015 in support of his candidature for a third term in office. The Proposal noted the need for the OECD to continue to strengthen its global reach and impact, bringing countries more closely to the OECD's policy standards.

A 2017 report on the Future Size and Membership of the OECD was undertaken for Council, which noted that six non-Members had expressed interest in membership and also recommended an evidence-based Framework that provided an objective benchmark to assess each prospective member on its respective merits and on a case-by-case basis. Council welcomed the Report, including the adoption of the Framework, and 'looked forward' to discussions on membership and a possible decision by July, 2017. However, it also noted, in a phrase that did not bode well for the July discussions, that it was not the size but the quality of the Organisation's work that would determine its impact and effectiveness.

In 2015, 2016 and 2017 Council encouraged the deepening of the OECD's relations with Sub-Saharan Africa, resulting in an increased range of developments, outlined in the 2018 'Mutual Engagement with Africa', report.

Enlargement

Council made two decisions to enlarge membership over 2007–2021, the first in 2007 regarding Chile, Estonia, Israel, the Russian Federation and Slovenia; the second in 2013 regarding Colombia and Latvia for that year, followed by Costa Rica and Lithuania in 2015. In both cases the discussions that led to the decisions were lengthy and often contentious as Members pursued national rather than OECD interests, despite the continuous encouragement of a Secretary-General very keen to see enlargement.

A roadmap was then developed for each of the nine candidates, listing the reviews to be undertaken in various policy areas in order to assess the country's position with respect to OECD instruments, standards and benchmarks, and identifying the OECD Committees and working groups to be involved in such reviews.

Chile, Estonia, Israel, and Slovenia had met the conditions for membership by the time of the MCM in May 2010 and acceded that year. However, Russia's progress became increasingly challenging, and was suspended in 2014, largely as a reaction to its annexation of the Crimea. What is described as technical co-operation between the OECD and the Russian Federation on topics of mutual benefit has, however, continued.

In 2012–2013 discussions continued on identifying candidates for accession, although, once again, it proved difficult to gain Members' agreement as to which countries should be selected. Finally, in 2013, Council agreed that accession discussions should commence with Colombia and Latvia that year, followed by Costa Rica and Lithuania in 2015. Rapid progress was made in achieving road map targets for Latvia and Lithuania, which became Members in 2016 and 2018, respectively, but progress was slower with Colombia, which achieved membership in 2020, and with Costa Rica, which is likely to accede in 2021, when total membership will be 38.

In 2016, the MCM established a working group of Ambassadors to once again consider the future size and membership of the Organisation, to report to the 2017 MCM. The Report was submitted and adopted by the MCM in 2017, having found that interest in membership was still strong, with six written requests for membership in 2017, and that Members felt that the OECD should continue to remain open to new Members, although also noting that the Organisation did not need to be universal to be effective.

The Report noted that the accessions of Lithuania, Colombia and Costa Rica would bring total membership to 38, with five countries (Brazil, China, India, Indonesia and South Africa) designated as Key Partners, with the possibility of accession at some future date. Six non-Members (Argentina, Brazil – both members of the

G20 – Bulgaria, Croatia, Peru and Romania), had at that time expressed interest in membership. The Report concluded that, based on these figures, the OECD's membership might reach 50, but that this was not a target or a ceiling. The working group made no suggestion as to which countries might be offered the possibility of accession, as no agreement had been reached between Members at this time. However, based largely on advice from the Secretariat, it did provide a more systematic and evidence-based framework for assessing whether or not to open accession discussions with a prospective Member, made public on the OECD website.

Decisions on new Members are, as might be expected, politically sensitive, focusing not only on whether possible candidates meet the specified criteria, but whether or not existing Members can gain concessions in other arenas, for example, in the WTO, in return for their support for a candidate. This has been evident in relation to Argentina, Brazil, Bulgaria, Croatia, Peru and Romania, the 'Prospective Members', where, four years after the OECD Council started discussing these countries' accession prospects, they had received no final reply as to the OECD's position on their accession, in spite of their progress in aligning with OECD policies and standards. This was despite the urgings of Secretary-General Gurría, for example in 2018, who stressed that a new round of enlargement should commence as soon as possible, particularly as progress on engagement had already been made by Argentina and Romania and that a 'window of opportunity', as he put it, seemed to have opened up in the case of Brazil.

The enlargement process has been constantly challenging and, to date, new Members have been drawn only from Eastern Europe and Latin America, with little sign of substantive consideration of drawing Members from other regions, despite the Council's interest in candidates from Southeast Asia. As the Secretary-General noted in 2020, discussions on a new enlargement round had been 'prolonged and contentious', with Members seemingly impervious to his passionate arguments for enlargement and disappointment that neither Brazil or Argentina would gain membership during his period in office.

Enhanced Engagement

The Council's 2007 call for Enhanced Engagement was aimed at gaining direct and active participation in the OECD's official bodies and Committees by Brazil, the People's Republic of China, India, Indonesia and South Africa, with the Secretary-General being asked to develop recommendations for Council on how to expand OECD's relations with a limited range of selected countries and with regions of strategic interest for Members. In light of its growing weight in the world economy, Southeast Asia was highlighted as a region of strategic priority 'with a view to identifying countries for possible membership'.

In the following years, the five countries were gradually integrated into OECD policy discussions, with the Organisation, where requested, providing support for their reform goals. The integration involved both the Secretary-General and Deputy Secretary-Generals developing contacts and undertaking activities in the countries, as well as the countries' participation in the OECD's regular work programme and Committees.

The call for Enhanced Engagement was reinforced in 2010 by the Council's 'Deepening Enhanced Engagement: Guidelines to Committees', based on Secretariat advice (Committees had been required to develop their own proactive strategies for the involvement of non-Member economies in their work, based on relevance and mutual benefit, by Council in July 2004). The Guidelines were drafted to ensure that the global relations strategies developed by the substantive Committees were more fully aligned with the priority given by Council to the Key Partners, Brazil, China, India, Indonesia and South Africa. The Guidelines were a response to progress reports that had noted that the five countries' participation in Committees had increased sharply since 2007, but that this increase took largely the form of more ad hoc observerships, rather than a deeper partnership. Several Committees had found that not all Enhanced Engagement partners were keen to participate, some because of a lack of capacity for such engagement, some for other reasons.

The Guidelines soon had a positive impact, with all Committees reviewing their global relations strategies and developing various plans or roadmaps for deeper engagement, such as the Committees for Fiscal Affairs, Insurance and Private Pensions, Financial Markets and the Territorial Development Committee. In 2012 it was decided to clarify what had become a rather confusing classification of non-Members in regard to Committees, with non-Members participating in the work of one or more subsidiary bodies to be referred to as Partners. These could be invited to participate as an Invitee, Participant or Associate, with each category subject to a variety of conditions designed to ensure the maximum of participation and mutual benefit. Committees wishing to involve Partners in their work were required to develop a Participation Plan, within the context of their Global Relations Strategy, to be approved by Council, with involvement as a Participant or Associate subject to the payment of a fee.

Invitations to become an Associate were to be based on an assessment of the candidate's policies and of its commitment to the OECD's goals, practices and standards, and by its adherence to at least the legal instruments defined for this purpose in the Participation Plan of the Committee(s). Associates were granted almost the full status of Members in relation to the relevant Committee(s), entitling them to participate in the full range of work, including in Committee bureaus and decision-making processes, on an ad personam basis. Where an Associate repeatedly failed to meet its obligations, including payment of fees, it could be suspended or, subject to Council's agreement, its membership terminated.

These changes were in addition to those OECD Part I and Part II bodies where Members and partner countries already had an equal status. As of 2020, these included the Development Centre (29 Partners out of a membership of 56), the Global Forum on Transparency and Exchange of Information for Tax Purposes (124 Partners out of a membership of 161), the Programme for International Student Assessment, PISA, (44 participating non-Members out of the 80 participants of the 2018 assessment cycle) and the International Transport Forum (23 Partners out of a membership of 60).

Also, in 2012 Council adopted new rules to make participation by Key Partners and other important economies in OECD bodies and projects less difficult, notably in the Base Erosion and Profit Shifting Project (BEPS), and the review of the OECD's corporate governance instruments, on a basis of equality with OECD Members, as appropriate.

In addition to greater integration at the OECD, policy discussions with the Key Partners took place increasingly frequently within the context of regional or global organisations, notably the G20, involving Secretary-General Gurría, OECD Sherpas and a range of other officials from a variety of Directorates as the G20 expanded its calls upon the work of the OECD. These have proved an effective means for promoting the relevance of OECD work, their association with the G20 adding further weight to the credibility and status of the Organisation in global economic governance.

Most of the OECD's substantive Committees had completed and approved their revised Global Relations Strategies in line with the Guidelines by 2012, and their engagement with the five Key Partners had both broadened and deepened, also assisted by growing relations with them in the context of the G20, with all five being members. While broadening and deepening, the engagement was variable, depending on the interests of each of the Key Partners, which were by no means identical. Their involvement in OECD Committees, for example, varied, with those involved with capital flows, environment, taxation and agriculture being among the most popular. An indication of the increased engagement was an increase in the fee revenue they contributed to the OECD, which rose from €2.3 million in 2012 to €4.0 million in 2013.

The years 2014–2015 saw a continued, deepening of engagement with the Key Partners, focused on the development of jointly agreed work programmes, with agreements reached with China and Indonesia, and discussions underway with Brazil, India and South Africa. Progress was most rapid with Brazil and South Africa as regards official Partnerships in OECD bodies and adherence to OECD legal instruments, largely a reflection of their earlier engagement with the OECD. The success of the OECD in expanding its global relations was clearly evident in the increasing number of adherents to its various Legal Instruments, rising from 362 in 2005 to 1121 in 2020 (see Table 6.1).

Table 6.1: Non-Member Adherence to OECD Legal Instruments.

	2005	2010	2015	2020
Total number of adherences	362	495	708	1121
Number of adherences into force	311	333	546	827

A jointly agreed work programme was achieved with Brazil in 2016, but programmes with India and South Africa proved more difficult to achieve. However, individual Committees, at variable rates, were increasingly successful in their engagement with Key Partners. The Committee on Fiscal Affairs, for example, by 2017 was the first to include all Key Partners as Participants, with 12 other Committees having at least one or more Key Partners as Participants or Associates at that time.

Rising international tensions from 2017, especially those involving the US and China, made relations with the Key Partners more difficult to achieve and deepen, although progress was still made. The dramatic onset and continuing impact of the COVID-19 pandemic since 2020 have made the maintenance and deepening of relations with Key Partners again more challenging, although the OECD's rapid and successful move to 'virtual' meetings reduced the pandemic's adverse impact.

While none of the Enhanced Engagement Partners (later 'Key Partners') has yet achieved membership of the OECD, the increased effort driving broader and deeper engagement in 2012–2020 has been successful, although the degree of progress, as might be expected, varies by Partner. Brazil, for example, as judged by its adherence to 99 OECD legal instruments and participation in 37, is the foremost of Partners, although several of these types of co-operation date from the 1990s. In contrast, China adheres to 9 OECD legal instruments and participates in 11 Committees (7 as an Associate), although its involvement with the OECD covers a shorter period.

Regional Approaches

The OECD has had a varying number of Regional Programmes, commencing in Southeast Europe then expanding to the Middle East and North Africa, Eurasia, Southeast Asia and Latin America, sometimes in co-operation with regional organisations, for example, APEC and ASEAN. The programmes have varied in content and importance, from comprehensive programmes such as MENA, to those with a more limited theme or focus, such as investment, anti-corruption, corporate governance and capacity building.

However, in 2006 the regional programmes were seen by the ERC for the most part as little more than lists of activities rather than systematically developed programmes within a global relations strategy. Following a review in 2006 by the ERC, supported by the Secretariat, a proposal that such programmes meet a set of minimum requirements and features was developed, together with a list of five, progressively less comprehensive models for regional approaches, being: comprehensive regional programmes (e.g. MENA and the Baltic Regional Programme); thematic regional programmes (e.g. the Investment Compact, and the NEPAD-OECD Africa Investment Initiative); thematic regional networks (e.g. the Anti-Corruption Networks and the Round-Tables on Corporate Governance); seminar series (e.g. for taxation, competition, and at the OECD Istanbul Centre for Private Sector Development); and one-off, time limited, ad-hoc initiatives. Approved by Council in December 2006, the proposal became operational in 2007, with the Secretariat responsible for ensuring that the regional approaches in the programmes of work for 2007–2008 and beyond were progressively implemented in compliance with the framework and provided with a time-limited mandate.

The Council's 2007 call for Enhanced Engagement lent greater weight to work on regional programmes, with its request that the Secretary-General develop recommendations on how to expand OECD's relations with regions of strategic interest for Members, and noted that, given its growing economic significance, Southeast Asia was a region of strategic priority. The 2011 Fiftieth Anniversary Vision Statement continued Council's emphasis on the enhancement of regional activities, including partnerships with other international and regional organisations, such as regional development banks. It reiterated Council's commitment to supporting and strengthening policy dialogue with Southeast Asia, Latin America, Southeast Europe, Eurasia, and sub-Saharan Africa, as well as the Middle East and North Africa, where, with the Arab Spring uprisings, the Vision Statement noted the OECD would do all it could to provide support for economic and social reform initiatives.

In practice, given the complexity involved, progress in implementing the 2006 framework for regional programmes was variable. For example, a decision to establish a comprehensive Southeast Asia Programme was not agreed until 2013, and launched in 2014, consisting of six regional policy networks on tax, good regulatory practices, investment policy and promotion, education and skills development, SMEs and public-private partnerships to support connectivity for infrastructure development. Council invited the Secretary-General 'to speedily implement' the Programme and to again explore and develop recommendations on how to further strengthen the regional component of the OECD's global relations, particularly in regard to Africa, Latin America and MENA.

OECD activities in Latin America had grown steadily since 2001, and especially from 2010, with the launch of the Latin America and the Caribbean (LAC) Investment Initiative. With the Council's prodding, it was felt that LAC could benefit from a framework for strategic direction, which later evolved in the Latin American and Caribbean Regional Programmes launched at the 2016 MCM meeting. The Organisation had also increased its activities in MENA countries since the Arab Spring of 2011, but these were largely on the basis of individual country projects, given the widely varying needs of the countries involved, with a comprehensive programme still some way off. However, at this time (2014–2015), no formal, comprehensive, regional programme existed for either region, but they were under consideration, and also one for Africa.

The Southeast Asia Regional Programme commenced in 2014 and developed well in the period to 2016, with growing collaboration with the ASEAN Secretariat and the Economic Research Institute for ASEAN and Southeast Asia (ERIA) in Jakarta, with the new OECD Jakarta Office facilitating higher-level political engagement and providing greater visibility for OECD work. The collaboration with ASEAN aimed at strengthening support for the ASEAN economic integration process.

In 2016 the Latin America and the Caribbean Regional Programme (LACRP) was established to provide a regional, whole-of-government framework for the OECD's support for policy reform, focused on three priorities: increasing productivity, enhancing social inclusion and strengthening institutions and governance, as well as encouraging greater adherence to OECD legal instruments. As with the Southeast Asia Programme, there was a growing involvement with the United Nations Economic Commission for Latin America and the Caribbean (UN-ECLAC), the Inter-American Development Bank (IDB), the Development Bank of Latin America (CAF), the Organization of American States (OAS), the Ibero-American Secretariat (SEGIB), and the EU-LAC Foundation and the Pacific Alliance, building on the long-established links of the OECD Development Centre.

Involvement with the MENA region, through the MENA-OECD Initiative on Governance and Competitiveness for Development, also grew in 2014–2016, strengthened in particular by the participation of the OECD in the Deauville Partnership in the G7, where the OECD proposed a 'Compact for Economic Governance', aimed at furthering policy dialogue and capacity development. The Initiative was given a new mandate for 2016–2020, and for 2021–2025, to focus on promoting regional integration and inclusive growth.

Developments in the Eurasia Competitiveness Programme (ECP, covering Central Asia, Eastern Europe and the South Caucasus), the Southeast Europe Programme and sub-Saharan Africa were more modest. The ECP aimed at supporting the implementation of reforms by encouraging the use of OECD policy standards and legal instruments. It was granted a new mandate for 2016–2020 and, again, for 2021–2025, to focus on helping Partners devise and implement policies to improve the business environment.

In 2015 the MCM had called on the OECD to strengthen its regional programme with South East Europe and, in response, it was decided to enhance its role as a platform for strategic dialogue, focused on organising high-level events to review the Organisation's achievements, and to discuss the ways to increase the OECD's visibility and impact on economic reforms in South East Europe. Engagement with sub-Saharan Africa was also slowly developing, drawing on the expertise and contacts of the OECD's Development Cluster and the NEPAD-OECD Africa Investment Initiative, with the goal of including greater participation by countries in the region in the substantive Committees.

At the time of writing, 2021, the OECD regional programmes have continued to develop, despite the impact of COVID, providing an efficient means for using existing regional structures to disseminate OECD policies, standards and recommendations among a large number of countries. Increasingly, they have taken the form of Comprehensive Regional Programmes,with mandates from the Council or the External

Relations Committee. The Programmes may be modified to varying extents to incorporate lessons learnt in dealing with the COVID-19 pandemic.

International Organisations

The OECD and its predecessor have a variety of relationships with other international organisations, global and regional, some long established, such as those with the EEC/EU (see Chapter 6 Going National), and the UN, others more recent, such as that with the G20. Aiming to build on the increasingly successful relationships established with the G7/8 and the G20, in 2011 Secretary-General Gurría stressed the need to improve external relationships, arguing that the OECD should help strengthen multilateralism, and create an expanded network of countries and partners to improve policy making and implementation worldwide. What he described as a 'new multilateralism', should have the overarching goal of 'Better Policies for Better Lives' – the welfare of all citizens. This was a theme he came back to on several occasions, such as in 2018, when he proposed the creation of a network for co-operation on policy coherence, bringing together the international organisations involved in the G20 (IMF, World Bank, FSB, ILO, WTO and OECD). The objective would be to improve co-ordination and exchange of information among international organisations and multilateral fora, helping design and implement better policies for better lives.

In the context of the Global Relations Strategy, the OECD's relations with international organisations and multilateral fora are means to disseminating its policies and legal instruments on a regional and global basis, building on existing organisational frameworks and relationships, often with the assistance of Members that are also members of the other organisations. These relations also contribute to the objective of playing a meaningful role in global economic governance, within the guidelines established by the OECD Council, working jointly with one or more organisations to better develop, coordinate and implement global policies and standards. Among the more important regional organisations the OECD works with are APEC, ASEAN, Pacific Alliance, Union for the Mediterranean and, most of all, the EU.

In the remainder of this section, lack of space confines our examination primarily to OECD relations with the UN, the G7/8 and the G20.

The OECD and the United Nations

The signatories to the OEEC Convention, signed in Paris in 1948, were well aware of the importance of relationships between the OEEC and other international organisations, as were those who established its successor, the OECD. Hence, as with most of the new international bodies established in the years after 1945, Article 13 of the OEEC's Convention empowered the Organisation to enter into agreements with and make recommendations to international organisations. Article 20 went further, instructing it to 'establish such formal or informal relationships with the United Nations, its principal organs and subsidiary bodies and with the Specialised Agencies, as may best facilitate collaboration in the achievement of their respective aims'. While the OECD's Convention makes no specific mention of the UN or its agencies, in practice it continued to build upon the established relationship with the UN. In 1971, for example, the UN's Economic and Social Council (ECOSOC), extended a standing invitation to the OECD to be represented by an observer at Council sessions and to participate, but not to vote, in debates on questions of concern to the OECD. In 1998 the UN's General Assembly similarly invited the OECD to participate as an observer in its sessions and work.

In 2007, the OECD identified 68 international organisations with which it had one or more actual or planned relationships. Twenty-one of these, excluding the specialised agencies, were in the UN family, nearly a quarter of the total. The Statistics and Data Directorate, for example, had relationships with seven UN bodies. Among the most frequent, persistent and regular of the linkages have been those with the United Nations Development Programme (UNDP) and the IMF, though the extent and nature of the relationships have varied over time. They include, for example, the co-ordination and implementation of development assistance, with the OECD Directorates often making use of the field-level experience of UNDP staff. UNDP officials gain experience in specialised areas of OECD work, such as anti-corruption monitoring and assessment, and there are joint events, including specialised seminars and training courses.

OECD Directorates and committees also work closely with the UN's regional commissions. The OECD Committee on Statistics and Statistical Policy, for example, considers it essential that the OECD statistical activities be jointly organised with organisations such as Eurostat and the UN Economic Commission for Europe. It also jointly organises statistical activities with the UN Economic Commissions for Latin America and the Caribbean and Asia and the Pacific, especially to improve the knowledge and the use of OECD statistical standards. The OECD also supports the PARIS21 consortium and its activities to strengthen statistical capacities in developing countries. The Organisation works closely with the UN, IMF and World Bank to co-ordinate efforts and share knowledge on international tax matters, including a joint OECD-UNDP Tax Inspectors Without Borders Initiative that is estimated to have delivered over $500m in additional tax revenue for developing countries.

The United Nations General Assembly adopted the 2030 Agenda for Sustainable Development in September 2015, strongly supported by the OECD which, in 2016, established a Permanent Observer to both the General Assembly and ECOSOC in New York. The Council also holds an important annual meeting of Members and partners to discuss progress on the 2030 Agenda, together with a wide range of governments and international organisations.

More recent developments in the relationship include the UN's invitation for the OECD to participate in the 2019 and 2020 High Level Political Forums (HLPF) on Sustainable Development, the latter focused on financing for development in relation to the Sustainable Development Goals at which Secretary-General Gurría spoke alongside the UN Secretary-General and other leaders, bringing perspectives from the OECD on the theme of effective multilateralism in the face of the COVID-19 crisis. The OECD also works closely with the UN, IMF and World Bank to co-ordinate efforts and share knowledge on international tax matters through the Platform for Collaboration on Tax, and the relationship with the UN includes work on their corporate services including a regular exchange of information on the COVID-19 situation.

The OECD-UN relationship reached new heights in March 2021, when the General Assembly endorsed a resolution by Australia, Colombia, Hungary, Niger, Republic of Korea, Saint Lucia, Slovak Republic and Spain, that welcomed the strengthening of cooperation and coordination with the OECD and also noted the UN's conviction that the relationship would help achieve the aims of both organisations. It also requested the Secretary-General to report to the General Assembly at its 77th session on the implementation of the resolution.

From the G7/G8 to the G20

As noted in Chapter 3, and described at greater length in Chapter 4, the development of the G7 posed a challenge for the OECD, given that (with the exception of Russia, when the G7 became the G8), all G7 members were also in the OECD. The G7 had no formal status within the OECD but, given the political and economic power of the G7 Members in the OECD, and the fact that the bulk of the OECD's budget came from G7 Members, its actual status and influence were considerable. The power of what became the G7 Members had always been recognised by the smaller powers in the OECD, though their interests were protected to some degree by the requirement for consensus. From that perspective, the only difference, albeit an important one, was that the non-G7 members now had a somewhat reduced opportunity to influence the G7 Members, given that the latter also met outside the OECD.

However, despite Secretary-General van Lennep's fears, the relationship with the G7/G8 has been largely positive and the role of the Secretariat in its work has grown, culminating with the OECD being invited to the G7/G8's meetings in 2007. The relationship, strongly encouraged by Secretary-General Gurría since taking up office, with his very active participation, reached a new level at the Heiligendamm (2007) and L'Aquila (2009) summits, where the OECD was invited to provide the platform for dialogue with Brazil, India, China, Mexico and South Africa, who had been invited to the summit for the first time. The platform took the shape of the Heiligendamm/L'Aquila Support Unit, based at the OECD, under the direct supervision of Secretary-General Gurría.

However, the relationship with the G7/G8 faded into the background somewhat with the dramatic onset of the Global Financial Crisis (GFC) and the increasingly influential G20, although it soon reasserted itself as G7 members began to use it as a forum to discuss issues and approaches that were difficult in the G20. The G20 changed almost overnight from a finance ministers' forum set up to deal with the Asian Financial Crisis, to a leaders' forum that took on responsibility for coordinating and implementing the global response to the GFC. As with all of the 'Gs', the G20's lack of a secretariat for developing and implementing policy required cooperation with a range of international organisations, notably the IMF, the World Bank and, most of all, the OECD.

With the G20 leaders acutely aware of the need for organisational support in developing and implementing its decisions, especially if it was to maintain credibility, Secretary-General Gurría saw an opportunity to reinforce the impact and influence of the OECD's reputation at a time when there was concern that these were declining. After extensive and successful lobbying at the third G20 in Pittsburgh in September 2009, at the height of the GFC, the OECD secured endorsement for the further development of its regime for tax information exchange (see Chapter 4 on leadership and Chapter 10 on taxation for more details). This was helped by the fact that the OECD's well-regarded tax work had been stimulated by the G7's 1996 decision to request the OECD to develop measures to counter the distorting effects of harmful tax competition.

This endorsement by the G20, combined with the expertise of the OECD in tax work, led to rapid and significant progress in international tax regulation, led by the OECD. It was soon accompanied by a rapid expansion of G20-related work at the OECD, several times in co-operation with the ILO, IMF, World Bank, UNCTAD and the WTO. The organisation now provides:

- Assistance in defining the G20 agenda
- Policy options supported by evidence-based analysis and reports
- Help in forging consensus among G20 members in relation to priorities
- Strengthening global governance by developing and expanding its regulatory standards on a range of key issues, notably taxation
- Monitoring commitments from G20 meetings

Among more recent developments at the G20 led by the OECD, or based largely on its work, have been the G20 AI Principles, based on the OECD Recommendation on Artificial Intelligence; the development of the G20 Principles for Quality infrastructure Investment; and the G20 discussions on adapting to an ageing society. From March 2020, the Organisation has supported the design and implementation of the G20 response to the COVID crisis, by contributing to the G20 Finance Ministers and Central Bank Governors' Action Plan. It has also monitored, jointly with the ILO, the impact of COVID-19 on employment.

Secretary-General Gurría continues to participate in the 'Leaders' Summits' of the G20, supported by the OECD Sherpa and Sherpa office, and the Chief Economist in her capacity as OECD's G20 Finance Deputy. The Sherpa and his Office undertake the bulk of the OECD's preparatory work for each of the Summits, usually starting over a year before a Summit takes place.

Other Country Programmes

By the end of the first decade of the twenty-first century, it became clear that the Global Relations Strategy was deficient as regards actual or possible relationships with individual countries interested in aligning with OECD standards and legal instruments. Earlier, it had been possible for an interested country to do this on a case-by-case basis, without full consideration of its strategic value or benefit from the OECD's perspective.

In 2011, the Secretary-General proposed to Council a new approach that would identify medium to long-term objectives for countries keen to align with OECD standards, in the context of a country programme, even where they had little or no interest in full Membership. Each programme, agreed between the OECD and the country concerned, would have a fixed term mandate including provisions for multi-year funding and governance. The funding was to be obtained from voluntary contributions and grants, including a financial commitment from the country.

As of 2020, Country Programmes had been completed with Kazakhstan, Morocco and Peru, and assessed by Members as achieving mutually beneficial progress. In addition, a Country Programme with Thailand is underway and, in 2019, Council invited Egypt and Viet Nam to develop similar Programmes, with Tunisia and Ukraine expressing interest.

The Global Activities of Senior Management

While much of the detailed activity necessary to implement the Global Relations Strategy was carried out by staff within the Directorates and, increasingly, by the Global Relations Secretariat, it was often either preceded, or reinforced by the efforts of senior members of the Secretariat as they worked to initiate and strengthen relations with governments and international organisations not always enthusiastic about developing closer relations with the OECD.

As well as frequent meetings in Paris with visiting senior officials, the Secretary-General completed 631 overseas visits in 2007–2020 for example, where he engaged in hundreds of formal and informal meetings with many leaders and key stakeholders. These trips included his participation in the main international summits. The purpose of most of the visits was to present OECD policy advice to the respective countries, or to respond to requests for visits from Member and partner countries. In 2019, for example, he attended over 650 formal bilateral meetings, including 66 formal meetings with heads of state or government, 22 meetings with heads of international organisations and 184 meetings with ministers, as well as numerous informal interactions with high-level officials and senior stakeholders.

In relation to the G20, in 2019 alone, the Secretary-General was invited to participate in all high-level G20 meetings under the Japanese Presidency. These included the G20 Leaders' Summit in Osaka and the G20 Finance Ministers Meeting in Fukuoka. He also attended major meetings of the G7 in France, such as the G7 Leaders' Summit in Biarritz, the G7 Environmental Ministerial Meeting in Metz and the G7 Finance Ministers and Central Bank Governors Meeting in Chantilly. While not to the same extent, the Deputy Secretary-Generals undertook similar, overseas activities.

As the OECD's External Auditor found in a 2018 report, such visits by OECD officials are far more than mere 'jaunts' and, moreover while there has been, as expected, a rapid growth in overseas missions, it was driven largely by an increase in voluntary contributions. In comparing them with similar expenditures by other international organisations, those of the OECD were found to be typical, with no striking anomalies.

Given the above, it comes as no surprise that the extent of resources devoted to the Global Relations Strategy has increased dramatically since the early days of Gurría's period in office. In 2008, the CCNM had a total of 11 staff, with a budget of €1,605,000. In 2020 the budget for the Global Relations Secretariat was €19,514,000 (with 86% from voluntary contributions), with approximately 97 staff.

Conclusion

The policy of 'Going Global' and its impact has been the greatest success of Secretary-General Gurría and the officials of the OECD over not just the last 10, but 20 years. The policy has been guided by an increasingly comprehensive, but flexible, and evolving Global Relations Strategy. It is a policy and aligned strategy whose implementation has achieved a marked increase in the relevance, profile and standing of the OECD, constantly encouraged by a Secretary-General committed to the achievement of these goals, and with the capacity to motivate staff by the example set by his passion, energy and clearly-articulated vision. The OECD has become, in line with its Fiftieth Anniversary Vision Statement, the centre of a global policy network, with its standards and practices spreading on a global, participative basis to help ensure that globalisation takes place within an equally global system of standards and, where appropriate, regulations.

OECD in Pictures

Figure 1: General Marshall on the day of the Marshall Plan speech. 5 June 1947. ©OECD.

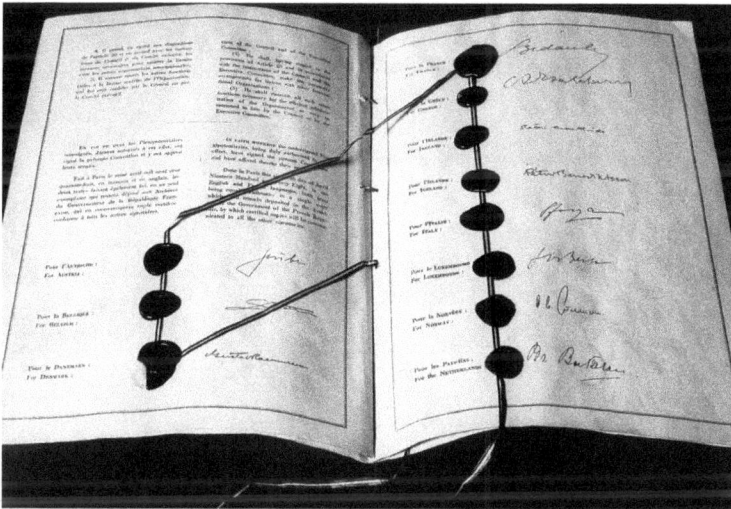

Figure 2: The Charter of the OEEC. ©OECD.

Figure 3: The Marshall Plan in Action. 1951. ©OECD.

Figure 4: Signing of the OECD Convention. 14 December 1960. ©OECD.

Figure 5: The first OECD Ministerial Council Meeting. 17 November 1961. ©OECD.

Figure 6: The first meeting of the OECD Environment Committee at Ministerial Level. 13-14 November 1974. ©OECD.

Figure 7: US President, Jimmy Carter and OECD Secretary-General, Emile Van Lennep. 5 January 1978. ©OECD.

Figure 8: Seminar "Women - Local Initiatives - Job Creation". 31 May 1985. ©OECD.

Figure 9: OECD Ministerial Council Meeting under the Chair of Mexico. 26 May 1999. ©OECD.

Figure 10: Inauguration of the OECD Mexico Centre. 26 April 2000. ©OECD.

Figure 11: OECD Ministerial Council Meeting - 50th Anniversary. 25 May 2011. ©OECD.

Figure 12: OECD Ministerial Council Meeting - 50th Anniversary. 25 May 2011. ©OECD/Michael Dean.

Figure 13: Official Visit of the French President, François Hollande and Heads of International Organisations to the OECD. 29 October 2012. ©OECD/Herve Cortinat.

Figure 14: Official Family Photo of the 2011 OECD Ministerial Council Meeting. 25 May 2011. ©OECD/Jean-Pierre Pouteau.

Figure 15: Interim President of the Central African Republic, Catherine Samba- Panza, with OECD Secretary- General, Angel Gurría. 4 April 2014. ©OECD/ Michael Dean.

Figure 16: EU Trade Commissioner Karel de Gucht, OECD Secretary General Angel Gurría and WTO Director-General Pascal Lamy at the joint OECD-WTO press conference on the Trade in Value-Added Initiative (TIVA). OECD. 16 January 2013. ©OECD/Michael Dean.

Figure 17: Ursula von der Leyen, President of the European Commission, Bruno Le Maire, Minister of the Economy and Finance of France and Angel Gurría, OECD Secretary-General at the Davos World Economic Forum. 22 January 2020. ©OECD.

Figure 18: Sanna Marin, Prime Minister of Finland, and Angel Gurría, OECD Secretary-General at the Davos World Economic Forum. 23 January 2020. ©OECD.

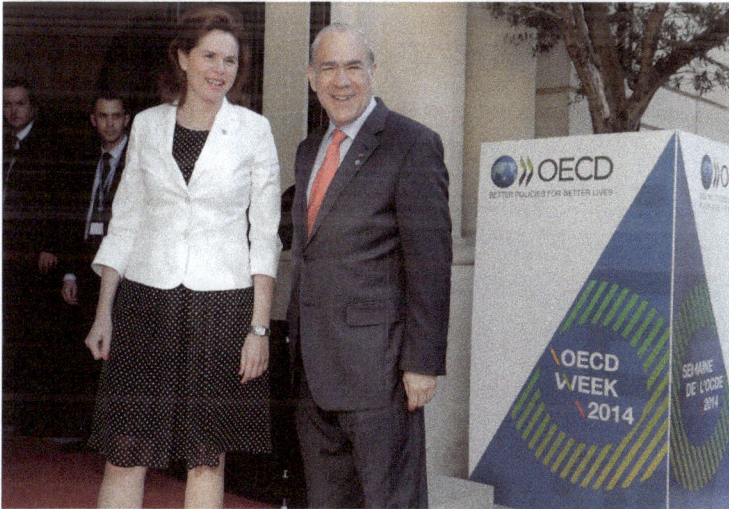

Figure 19: OECD Week 2014. Alenka Bratušek, Prime Minister of the Republic of Slovenia with the OECD Secretary-General, Angel Gurría. 5 May 2014. ©OECD/Victor Tonelli.

Figure 20: Official Family Photo of the 2015 OECD Ministerial Council Meeting. 3 June 2015. ©OECD/ Hervé Cortinat.

Figure 21: UN Secretary-General Ban Ki-moon visits the OECD. 28 April 2015. ©OECD/Matthieu de Martignac.

Figure 22: Official Visit of Li Keqiang, Premier of the People's Republic of China to the OECD. 1 July 2015. ©OECD.

Figure 23: Mark Rutte, Prime Minister of the Netherlands and Chair of the OECD Ministerial Council Meeting 2015 with OECD Secretary-General, Angel Gurría. 3 June 2015. ©OECD/Matthieu de Martignac.

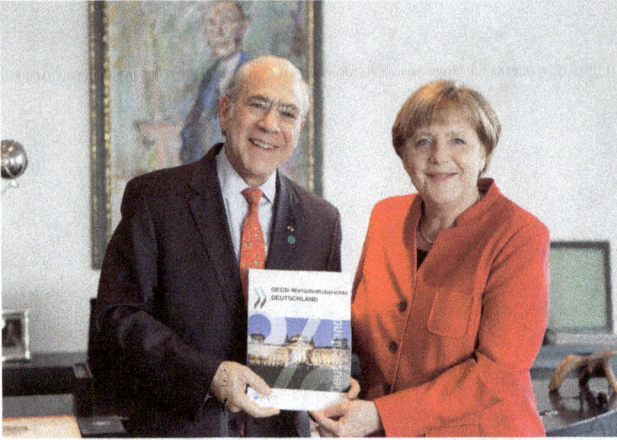

Figure 24: Presentation of the 2016 OECD Economic Survey of Germany. 5 April 2016. ©OECD/Axel Schmidt.

Figure 25: OECD and UNCTAD announce partnership on the new 2030 Agenda for Sustainable Development. UNCTAD Secretary-General Mukhisa Kituyi with OECD Secretary-General Angel Gurría. 25 September 2015. ©OECD/Catherine Bremer.

Figure 26 and 27: US President Barack Obama and OECD Secretary-General, Angel Gurría at the OECD. 1 December 2015. ©OECD/Julien Daniel.

Figure 28: U.S. President Barack Obama and OECD Secretary-General Angel Gurría. G7 Summit Ise Shima, Japan. 27 May 2016. © Jim Watson/AFP.

Figure 29: Jan Eliasson, Deputy Secretary-General, United Nations at the OECD 18 February 2016. ©OECD/Andrew Wheeler.

Figure 30: OECD Week 2018. Bilateral meeting with Mr. Māris Kučinskis, Prime Minister of Latvia. ©OECD/Julien Daniel.

Figure 31: Prime Minister Shinzō Abe of Japan with OECD Secretary-General Angel Gurría. Tokyo, Japan. 13 April 2017. ©Jiji Press.

Figure 32: ILO Director General, Guy Ryder with OECD Secretary-General Angel Gurría at the Meeting with Heads of International Organisations. 10 April 2017. ©OECD/Stefanie Loos.

Figure 33: OECD Week 2016. Michelle Bachelet, President of Chile with OECD Secretary-General, Angel Gurría. ©OECD/Julien Daniel.

Figure 34: Official Family Photo of the 2016 OECD Ministerial Council Meeting. 1st June 2016. ©OECD/Hervé Cortinat.

Figure 35: Nurhayati Ali Assegaf, Member of Parliament from Indonesia with OECD Secretary-General, Angel Gurría. Meeting of the OECD Global Parliamentary Network in Tokyo, April 2016. ©OECD.

Figure 36: Signing ceremony of OECD/UN Women Memorandum of Understanding (MOU). UN Women Executive Director Phumzile Mlambo- Ngcuka with OECD Secretary-General Angel Gurría. 17 September 2017. ©UN Women/Ryan Brown.

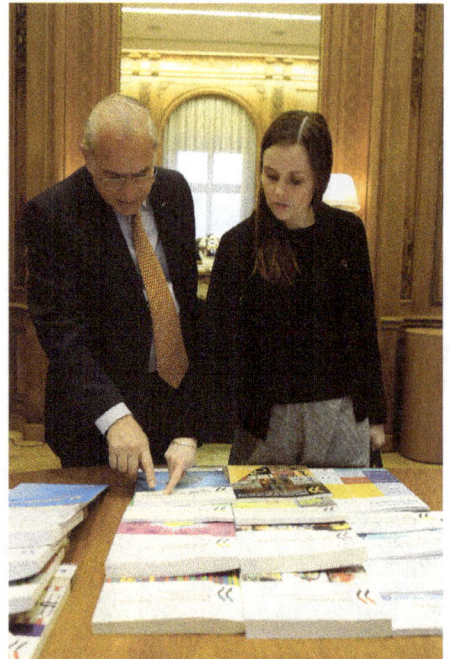

Figure 37: Katrín Jakobsdóttir, Prime Minister of Iceland with OECD Secretary-General Angel Gurría. 27 March 2018. ©OECD/Andrew Wheeler.

Figure 38: Prime Minister of Canada, Justin Trudeau, with OECD Secretary-General, Angel Gurría. Paris, France. 16 April 2018. ©OECD/Herve Cortinat.

Figure 39: French President Emmanuel Macron with OECD Secretary-General, Angel Gurría at the OECD. 26 April 2018. ©OECD/Victor Tonelli.

Figure 40: OECD Week 2018 - Signing Ceremony of Accession: Lithuania and Colombia
From left: Emmanuel Macron, President of France; Dalia Grybauskaitė, President
of Lithuania; Juan Manuel Santos, President of Colombia and Angel Gurría,
Secretary-General of the OECD. 30 May 2018. ©OECD/Julien Daniel.

Figure 41: OECD Forum 2018 - Arrival of Emmanuel Macron, President of France.
30 May 2018. ©OECD/Andrew Wheeler.

Figure 42: Meeting of Chancellor of Germany Angela Merkel with the Heads of International Organisations in Berlin. 11 June 2018. ©OECD Berlin/Hermann Bredehorst.

Figure 43: Global Deal Conference Opening with Mr. Stefan Löfven, Prime Minister of Sweden. 4 February 2020. ©OECD/Hervé Cortinat.

Figure 44: UN Secretary-General, António Guterres with OECD Secretary-General, Angel Gurría at the 73rd United Nations General Assembly. 24 September 2018. ©OECD.

Figure 45: UN Secretary-General, António Guterres with OECD Secretary-General, Angel Gurría. UN, New York. 20 September 2019. ©UN.

Figure 46: 60th Anniversary of the signing of the OECD Convention. 14 December 2020. ©OECD.

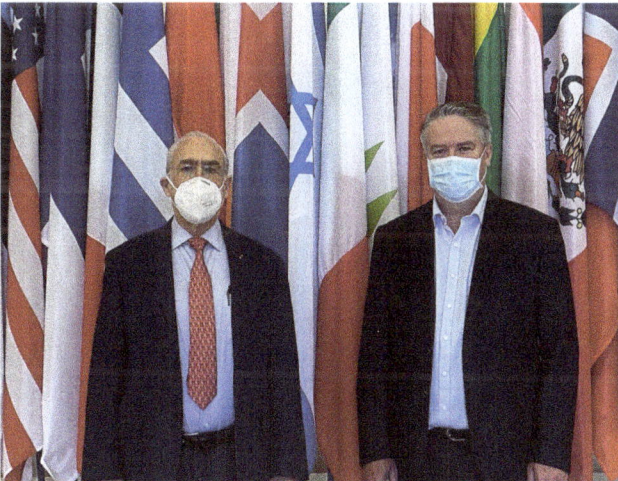

Figure 47: Angel Gurría, OECD Secretary-General with Mathias Cormann, incoming OECD Secretary-General. 3 May 2021. ©OECD.

7 Going Green

The OECD was created before the rise of environmental concerns in the late 1960s, but it has played an increasingly significant role in putting environmental issues at the heart of economic policy-making. As the OECD Environment Policy Committee marks its 50th anniversary, this chapter provides a brief account of some of that early work, before focusing on the development and application of the OECD's 2011 Green Growth Strategy in response to the Global Financial Crisis of 2008 – swimming against the tide that suggests economic growth and the environment are in opposition. It also examines in some detail the OECD's contributions to the development of the international climate change regime, before providing some account of other activity in 2010–2021.

Environment Activities in the OECD

Sir Alexander King, who was then Director-General for Scientific Affairs at the OECD, together with the Italian industrialist Aurelio Peccei, in 1968 founded the Club of Rome which, after a faltering beginning, published the *Limits to Growth* study in 1972 – a substantial challenge to the thinking underlying the post-war 'long boom'. As Matthias Schmelzer put it, the Club of Rome was 'born in the corridors of the OECD'.

The emergence of environmental concerns led the Organisation to establish an Environment Committee in 1970 (later renamed Environment Policy Committee), serviced by a new Environment Directorate, that would integrate the work of environmental and economic policies and started work as of January 1971. The aim was to produce work that would assist in the reduction of pollution, the assessment of environmental performance, the development of environmental protection tools, and improve the quantity and quality of international data and information on environmental issues.

This activity has continued to develop and has been of considerable value in producing conceptual work that has been impactful in Member and non-member countries alike, and in other international settings. The OECD formulated the Polluter Pays Principle, the principle that polluters should be charged for the costs of their action, which has had a far-reaching impact on policy thinking worldwide. The Principles of Good Laboratory Practice and the Mutual Acceptance of Data have also helped to prevent the use of differing regulatory risk regimes as disguised barriers to trade, and thus facilitated trade liberalisation in the chemicals industry. The OECD also developed much of the policy architecture underpinning the Basel Convention governing trade in hazardous waste in the wider multilateral system.

The OECD played an important role in the development of the 1979 Convention on Long-Range Transboundary Air Pollution. Research by Swedish scientists in the

https://doi.org/10.1515/9783110735833-007

late 1960s was followed by a call for international action issued by the 1972 Stockholm Conference. In this respect, the OECD undertook analytical and monitoring work from 1973 to 1978 before the Convention was negotiated within the UN Economic Commission for Europe (UNECE) and ultimately signed by 34 states, in both Europe and North America, under the auspices of UNECE.

The OECD also established links with several intergovernmental organisations. UNECE and the Council of Europe became observers at Environment Committee meetings in 1971. UNEP became an observer in 1974, followed by the WHO and the GATT, as the Organisation's environmental work took on greater significance for non-member countries. Technical co-operation also began with the Commission of the European Communities in the mid-1970s.

In the late 1970s, Members concerns focused on economic recession, unemployment and energy shortages, with the environment receding somewhat in the Organisation's priorities. Nevertheless, the Environment Committee generated 16 Council Acts between 1976 and 1979.

The Committee met in special session to reflect on the next decade of environmental action in April 1981, and held two workshops later that year which produced 11 issues papers to guide the work of the Committee on the following topics:
- CO_2 and climate change
- The ozone layer
- Acid precipitation
- Chemicals
- International movement of hazardous wastes
- Maintaining biological diversity
- Loss of cropland and soil degradation
- Environmental aspects of bilateral development assistance
- Environmental impact assessment and international co-operation
- Environmental aspects of multinational investment
- International application of the 'polluter pays' principle

The initiation of work on climate change at such an early stage is rather underacknowledged. The First World Climate Conference was held only in February 1979 and at the Second Meeting of the Environment Committee at Ministerial Level, held on 7–8 May 1979, Ministers considered both stratospheric ozone depletion and climate change.

A joint OECD and IEA experts workshop on CO_2 Research and Assessment, in February 1981, recommended further such meetings to examine the state-of-the-art of climate change, and provide guidance on policy options. This workshop was therefore instrumental in encouraging the Organisation to become more heavily involved in climate change issues. In the latter half of the 1980s, work on climate change in the OECD picked up substantially, with the USA and Canada being particularly active – Canada making an (unsuccessful) attempt to recruit the OECD to the 1988 Toronto climate conference.

The OECD also played a significant part in the development of the UN Framework Convention on Climate Change from 1990 onwards. Specifically, it provided analyses that were incorporated into the Convention, since the Intergovernmental Negotiating Committee (INC) lacked any capacity for such work. As UNFCCC did not enter into force until 1995, much of the work underpinning the development of the Kyoto Protocol was also performed by the OECD, as well as the OECD/IEA Climate Change Experts Group.[1] One such contribution was the production in 1989 of a modelling study of the costs of various climate change response strategies that led to the subsequent development by the Economic and Statistics Department of an applied general equilibrium model called 'GREEN'. Modelling using GREEN led to a stream of research on the economics of climate change during 1990–1992. The OECD also supported the work of the Intergovernmental Panel on Climate Change.

The Environment Committee had undertaken reviews of environmental policies, such as that on New Zealand in 1980 (at the request of the Government of New Zealand) and this was extended in 1992, at the request of Environment Minsters, to peer-reviewed Environmental Performance Reviews (EPR) which have now covered over 90 Member and partner countries.

The criticism that the OECD was an embodiment of 'neoliberalism' during this period is rather belied by the scope and depth of this work on the environment. The recent focus on 'Green Growth' puts that notion well to bed.

Green Growth

The historical work on the environment was followed by an even greater emphasis in the form of 'Green Growth' endorsed at the 2009 OECD Ministerial Council Meeting (MCM) as a strategy – along with a focus on innovation, to boost sluggish growth as the global economy emerged from the Global Financial Crisis. The MCM adopted a Declaration on Green Growth on 25 June 2009.

Policymakers globally were struggling with record unemployment, unsustainable fiscal deficits and low growth. At the same time, environmental concerns – especially climate change – were being seen as an increasingly important component of economic policy. Significantly, the Ministers had an eye on UNFCC COP-15 later in 2009, and aspired to play a positive role in preparing for a successful outcome, though this effort was to prove futile as that conference ended in failure. The Declaration on Green Growth stated that the OECD could, with its capacity for policy analysis and identification of best practices, assist countries to respond to the growing

---

1 Established in 1993 as the 'Annex I Experts Group'.

policy demands to foster green growth, and work with countries to develop further measures to build sustainable economies.

Ministers invited the OECD to develop the Green Growth Strategy, to achieve economic recovery with environmentally and socially sustainable economic growth. They called upon the Organisation and its Committees to prioritise work so as to support green growth policies. The Strategy's principal aim was to analyse green growth measures in OECD Member and major non-member countries. It was required to incorporate consideration of the OECD Innovation Strategy, the OECD Environmental Outlook to 2030, OECD work on the economics of climate change, the results of the Copenhagen UN Climate Change Conference of December 2009, and inputs from the IEA.

An interim report on progress in developing the Green Growth Strategy was required to be presented to the 2010 MCM, and the Organisation was requested to co-operate closely with non-OECD countries, the private sector, civil society and other international organisations. The Green Growth Strategy was delivered to, and adopted by, the 2011 MCM, as a key contribution of the OECD to the 'Rio+20' UN Conference on Sustainable Development in 2012. It proposed a flexible policy framework and a set of indicators that could be applied to various country circumstances.

The first Green Growth and Sustainable Development Forum (GGSD Forum) took place on 23 November 2012 and was attended by approximately 250 participants, including representatives from ministries of finance, economics, environment, development cooperation, sciences, industry and technology, and foreign affairs, as well as from international organisations, the private sector and civil society. The focus was on how to encourage a more efficient and sustainable use of natural resources, looking at the implications for advanced, emerging and developing countries. Stakeholders took the opportunity to exchange experiences and best practices with the management of natural resources. Since then, a total of nine GGSD Forums have taken place each year, focusing on a different issue.

The 'horizontal' programme to implement the Green Growth strategy across numerous OECD policy Committees has influenced most of the relevant 'vertical' programmes, including: Fiscal Policy and Green Growth; Green Finance and Investment; Trade and Green Growth; Innovation for Green Growth; and, Green Growth for Key Sectors: Energy, Transport and Agriculture. These activities have seen the conduct of several projects that have given rise to published documents, some more conceptual, such as Fostering Innovation for Green Growth, Towards Green Growth, and Developing Green Growth Indicators; some related to policy sectors, such as Mining and Green Growth, Building Resilient Cities, Improving Energy Efficiency in the Agro-food Chain, Farm Management Practices to Foster Green Growth, Green Growth in Fisheries and Aquaculture. Other projects have been country-specific, such as Addressing Industrial Pollution in Kazakhstan; or Boosting Skills for Greener Jobs in Flanders, Belgium.

In 2017, the horizontal work on Green Growth also led to the production of a policy paper, *Industrial Upgrading for Green Growth in China,* arising from a project undertaken jointly with the Development Research Centre of the State Council of China (DRC) on better alignment of industrial and environmental policies in China. The paper focused on promoting industrial restructuring, addressing challenges arising from China's 'New Productive Revolution' and improving the environmental and resource efficiency of the Chinese economy.

Green growth has been progressively mainstreamed in OECD Economic Surveys. The Economic Outlook has been increasingly providing advice on how short-term policy actions (fiscal, monetary) fit into a longer-term picture, in particular that of addressing environmental sustainability, as evidenced in the most recent OECD Interim Economic Outlook, launched on 9 March 2021. The environmental sustainability dimension was added in the 2019 *Going for Growth* edition, with a focus on climate change mitigation and air pollution, resulting in the inclusion of green growth among the top five priorities for countries' structural reform. The 2021 special COVID-19 Recovery *Going for Growth* edition identifies climate change as one of the top priorities that would benefit from international cooperation and coordination of policies.

The implementation of the Green Growth Strategy has therefore become central to the activities of the OECD, stretching across Committees and Directorates and developing significant relationships with non-members and other international policy arenas, such as the G7, G20 and UN regimes such as those on climate change and biodiversity. We will now discuss the strength of this contribution in relation to climate change, before noting some activities on other environmental policy issues.

Climate Change: From Kyoto to Paris and Beyond

After the conclusion of the Kyoto Protocol, the OECD continued its work on addressing climate change, focusing on supporting implementation and compliance. Together with the IEA, the OECD conducted analytical work for the 'Annex I Expert Group' established in 1993 and renamed as the Climate Change Expert Group (CCXG) in 2005. (Kyoto Protocol Annex I countries were the industrialized nations and countries with economies in transition).

The CCXG is a forum for promoting dialogue on and enhancing the understanding of technical issues in international climate change negotiations and climate policy implementation. The group typically meets bi-annually; holds Global Fora to bring together experts from developed and developing countries, the private sector and civil society; and develops technical papers in consultation with a wide range of countries. CCXG has influenced substantially the development of the international climate regime, developing guidelines adopted by the UNFCCC for the preparation of initial National Communications by Annex I countries. The CCXG can very much claim to have 'laid the groundwork' for the inclusion of emissions trading in the Kyoto Protocol, as well as developing the concept of a 'commitment period reserve', also adopted by the UNFCCC.

In the lead-up to COP21, CCXG research and analysis supported governments in the development of the 2015 Paris Agreement, focusing on three key areas: designing the elements of a 2015 agreement, climate finance, and a post-2020 accounting framework. The numerous reports produced between 2009 and 2015 provided key technical inputs to the UNFCCC negotiations and concretely impacted their outcomes. For example, CCXG work on transparency and measurement, reporting and verification (MRV) contributed to the agreement of an Enhanced Transparency Framework (ETF) that addressed some of the gaps in existing MRV systems. Work on mitigation contributions resulted in an increased emphasis of the Paris Agreement on providing information necessary for clarity, transparency and understanding of Nationally Determined Contributions (NDCs). Work on carbon markets contributed to Paris Agreement's inclusion of text on carbon markets, as well as of a new market mechanism under Article 6.

Secretary-General Gurría personally played a significant role in guiding OECD work on climate change. He was one of the first global leaders to call for zero emissions in the second half of the century, during a lecture in London in October 2013. Through his series of biennial climate lectures, beginning in 2013 and concluding in 2021, Gurría frequently insisted on 'putting a big fat price on carbon'.

He also played a significant role in the run-up to and at COP21 in Paris in 2015. In advance of COP21, the OECD presented the report, *Climate Finance in 2013–14 and the USD 100 billion Goal*, which was a first-of-its-kind assessment of progress towards the goal set in Copenhagen in 2009 for developed countries to mobilise USD 100 billion per year by 2020 for climate action in developing countries. In doing so, the OECD provided a critical contribution to the successful negotiations that led to the drafting and signing of the Paris Agreement. The OECD continues to monitor progress towards the 100 billion goal, the fulfilment of which remains of paramount importance for trust building and progress on other issues negotiated under the UNFCCC.

The OECD had a considerable presence at the COP21 in Paris and hired a large pavilion, hosting around 100 events, along with the International Energy Agency and the Nuclear Energy Agency. This was undoubtedly assisted by the fact that the COP was meeting in Paris, and would have been more difficult for the OECD had it not been conducted in its home city.

After COP21, CCXG work focused on supporting governments in the implementation of the Paris Agreement. In the last few years, CCXG has produced analysis to support the implementation of the Enhanced Transparency Framework of the Paris Agreement, focusing particularly on technical aspects related to the reporting of financial support, GHG inventories and progress towards Nationally Determined Contributions (NDCs). A substantive part of CCXG work has also focused on technical issues relevant to operationalising Article 6 of the Paris Agreement. In 2019, the

CCXG produced work to support countries in preparing their long-term low greenhouse gas emission development strategies and in strengthening the linkages between a long-term vision and NDCs. In 2020, CCXG and EPOC work has focused on enhancing the understanding of how governments' responses to the COVID-19 crisis could be implemented so as to improve the climate, environment and broader wellbeing. By engaging the OECD membership who account for a majority of emissions of GHGs, as well as drawing in a large number of developing countries, this has undoubtedly helped build agreement on key elements of policies that later have been adopted elsewhere.

The work was undertaken by only about half a dozen staff, and it received the plaudits of the UN Secretary-General and the French host. The new emphasis on climate finance under the Paris Agreement would have been difficult to undertake from funds from the regular Part I budget, but it was made possible by the provision of voluntary contributions from Germany and others, and the Secretary-General also made funds available for work on mitigation, which had been neglected previously relative to other activities. Prior to 2015 there was no 'mitigation team'.

Voluntary contributions provided continuing support for work on climate finance by Members for various activities, including the significant contribution of the OECD to the development of the Paris Agreement. The change of administrations in the US underscored this. The Obama Administration was strongly supportive of the contribution to the Paris Agreement; the Trump Administration, however, limited the progress the OECD could make from 2017 onwards. The 'mutual agreement' decision rule meant that opposition, or even a lack of enthusiasm, could act as an important brake on the development of such work programmes.

This constraint, however, does not always make for bad outcomes. One example was the attempt by the US, under President Obama, to prohibit the use of export credits for the financing of coal-fired power stations in 2015 (before the Paris Agreement was concluded). The US had already pushed through such a ban in the World Bank the previous year, with the Adoption of a Directions Statement to that effect – reflecting the quasi-hegemonic position of the US in the Bank. (The quantum of finance from export credits was in fact larger than that from the Bank). The Participants to the Arrangement on Officially Supported Export Credits in the OECD (especially Australia, a coal exporter, and Korea, a technology exporter) failed to support such a ban, and compromise saw a continuation of export credits permitted for High Efficiency Low Emissions technology, which can provide reductions in greenhouse gas emission of 25% and more per unit of electricity generated over the existing coal-fired fleet. Support for even less efficient plants was permitted in developing countries. Aside from limiting restrictions on the development of less affluent countries, the resulting compromise also limited the scope for China to fill the vacuum created. It has expanded considerably its financing of less efficient plants, and thus its influence, but the ban the US proposed would have handed to it greater opportunities.

The relationship continued with the G20, which, like the G7, lacked any analytical capacity itself independent of members. In preparation for the G20 meeting in Germany in July 2017, the OECD produced a report for the German presidency, *Investing in Climate, Investing in Growth*, with analysis suggesting that, rather than treating climate as a separate issue, integrating the growth and climate agendas could add 1% to average economic output in G20 countries by 2021 and increase output by up to 2.8% by 2050. It also estimated that if the benefits of avoiding impacts such as coastal flooding or storm damage were factored in, the net increase to 2050 GDP could be almost 5%.

Together with the German Ministry of Environment, Nature Conservation, Building and Nuclear Safety, the OECD hosted an international conference in Berlin, in collaboration with the Petersberg Climate Dialogue, to launch the study. The conference was attended by decision-makers from many countries, business representatives and high-level actors from other international organisations. The OECD was thus well-placed in the global climate change policy network, and the Environment Directorate also took part in the Technical Expert Group of the Sustainable Financial Group for the European Union. Germany's voluntary funding for the study also helped raise awareness on the importance of the climate change issue in the Economics Department, which had previously not been as well integrated with climate activities as it had been within other OECD departments, for example, the Development Assistance Committee and the Committee on Fiscal Affairs, under which the Centre for Tax Policy had undertaken work on carbon pricing and environmental taxation.

The OECD's work on climate change has also taken strides to move beyond mitigation to include more work on adaptation. Adaptation to climate change has long been the 'poor relation' to mitigation, and it was marginalised from the agenda of the Framework Convention from the outset, at the insistence of NGOs and those parties who saw an opportunity in the demand for the primacy of action on mitigation.

In 2016, the OECD established a Centre on Green Finance and Investment, leveraging its policy and economics expertise and enabling knowledge exchange among leaders from the private sector, government and regulatory institutions, academia, and civil society through its annual Forum on Green Finance. It also supported the development of the French-led proposal to establish the International Programme for Action on Climate (IPAC) to facilitate collaboration across Committees and the broader OECD family (IEA, NEA and ITF) to create an annual assessment of countries' progress towards net-zero targets, based on policy indicators, and providing targeted advice and sharing of best practice. IPAC was approved by the OECD Council in April 2021.

In addition, the OECD's horizontal project Building Climate and Economic Resilience in the Transition to a Low-Carbon Economy is focused on improving economic and climate resilience in the context of fostering a recovery from the COVID-19 crisis.

As part of the effort to help countries achieve a green recovery, the OECD Secretariat has also been developing, updating and refining a database tracking the environmental dimensions of recovery measures announced by OECD and key partner countries. The aim is to provide countries and the public with a comprehensive overview of announced recovery measures that are likely to have significant environmental implications.

Recent Work Beyond Climate Change

The work of the OECD on environmental issues other than climate change has also expanded. Work on biodiversity, for example, was under-represented for a long time, with a single staff member in the Environment Directorate allocated to this issue. The G7 meeting in 2019 (hosted by France) however, saw a recognition of the economic and business case for action on biodiversity. The OECD thus produced a report to feed into the G7, *Biodiversity: Finance and the Economic and Business Case for Action*. On 4 December 2015, the Financial Stability Board, of which the OECD is a member, established an industry-led Taskforce on Climate Related Financial Disclosures (TCFD), and in 2020 the model was extended to biodiversity and natural capital with the establishment of a Taskforce on Nature-related Financial Disclosures (TNFD) by UNEP, UNDP and a number of civil society partners.

The TNFD is the result of a partnership between Global Canopy, the United Nations Development Programme (UNDP), the United Nations Environment Programme Finance Initiative (UNEP FI), and the World Wide Fund for Nature (WWF). It was conceived in January 2019 at the World Economic Forum, after the French Government commissioned a report from AXA and WWF calling for such a mechanism in May 2019. Another high-level Roundtable was held at the Davos World Forum in January 2020. It has been developed outside the auspices of the OECD, but the Organisation is supporting the initiative, and sees that a contribution can be made to its objectives by the uptake of the standards and tools of responsible business conduct (RBC), the OECD's Guidelines for Multinational Enterprises and OECD Due Diligence Guidance for Responsible Business Conduct. It will also be assisted by the Paris Collaborative on Green Budgeting, launched by the OECD at the One Planet Summit in 2017 (with the support of France and Mexico), which seeks to design new tools to assess and align government budgets and fiscal policies with environmental objectives, including those on climate and biodiversity.

In recent years, focus on water policy (a particular interest of Secretary-General Gurría) has also expanded. Specifically, a Roundtable on Financing Water was established in April 2017, a joint initiative of the OECD, the World Water Council, the Netherlands and the World Bank. The Roundtable facilitates dialogue between the water and finance policy communities, with a focus on meeting the global challenges of financing the investments needed for water security and sustainable economic growth, and the contribution of water to the Sustainable Development Goals. The Roundtable also provides a global multi-stakeholder platform for key actors in the water and finance sectors. It brings together a range of government representatives in developed, emerging and developing economies, as well as institutional investors, private industry, international organisations, philanthropic organisations, academia and civil society organisations.

The OECD has also placed an increased emphasis on ocean issues in recent years. The Environment Directorate has brought formerly horizontal work together under one umbrella to communicate it cohesively. Substantive joint work on the oceans has also increased, for example through the Sustainable Ocean for All report published in 2020, and work on ocean finance and on ghost fishing gear for the UK G7 Presidency.

Last but not least, the OECD organises the annual Private Finance for Sustainable Development (PF4SD) Conference, bringing together relevant stakeholders from the public and private sectors of developed and developing countries to discuss new approaches in financing the 2030 Agenda for Sustainable Development.

Conclusion

The OECD has addressed environmental policy issues since the very emergence of concern over such matter in the late 1960s and early 1970s. The OECD work on environment might have been challenged by the Global Financial Crisis of 2008 as environmental policy has tended traditionally to be viewed as being in opposition to economic growth. Rather than being constrained by this older thinking, the OECD under Secretary-General Gurría adopted the Green Growth Declaration in 2009 and the 2011 Green Growth Strategy on the premise that 'going green' can spur new sources of growth. This development was encouraged by the support at various stages by member states such as France, Germany and the United Kingdom, and was assisted by the Obama Administration in the US, which was more conducive to these initiatives than its successor, the Trump Administration.

The OECD can no longer be regarded as a bastion of neoliberal economics to the neglect of concerns related to the natural environment and social concerns. Just how bold the work programme is can be seen when one considers that its work on the economics of biodiversity loss is based on the results of modelling habitat loss (through the application of the species-area model), applying the results of climate impact models, and using the outcomes from climate (general circulation) models, employing various emissions scenarios as inputs.

It can no longer be said that the OECD is so committed to economic thinking that it neglects the environment.

8 From GDP to Well Being, Inclusive Growth, Education

On its 50th anniversary in 2011 the OECD launched *How's Life?*, a statistical report that has been released biennially since, to promote the OECD's mission, captured by the slogan 'Better Policies for Better Lives'. This was part of the OECD's Better Life Initiative, which also includes the 'Your Better Life Index', an interactive composite index of well-being designed to involve citizens in the debate on societal progress.

How's Life? captures some essential aspects of life affecting well-being in OECD and partner countries, based on a framework covering 11 dimensions of current well-being and four resources for future well-being. The report describes how well-being is changing over time and how it is distributed among different groups in each population.

The OECD has the objective, embedded in its Convention, of maximising sustainable economic growth. But as the *How's Life?* initiative suggests, it has more recently reflected a belief that the well-being of citizens rests on more than just maximising Gross Domestic Product – either in absolute terms or even in per capita terms. *How's Life?* commenced before the effects of the Global Financial Crisis (GFC) really became evident, but which supported even more after the GFC raised questions about inequalities in OECD Member countries. As well as the work on well-being, this chapter also describes initiatives to tackle inequalities, as exemplified by the Growing Unequal and Framework for Policy Action on Inclusive Growth projects; and the relation of these to work on education and skills.

The Origins of the Better Life Initiative

The adequacy of GDP as a measure of economic welfare had been questioned for some time, and in February 2008 the French President Nicolas Sarkozy established a commission to explore this issue – the Commission on the Measurement of Economic Performance and Social Progress (CMEPSP), sometimes referred to by the surnames of its leaders as the Stiglitz-Sen-Fitoussi Commission. CMEPSP was closely connected to the OECD, as among its membership were Enrico Giovannini, Chief Statistician and Director of the Statistics Directorate, and Jean-Philippe Cotis, who had only recently stepped down as Chief Economist and Head of the Economics Department. Two members of the OECD Secretariat were rapporteurs for the Commission.

The Commission made 12 recommendations including: when evaluating material well-being, look at income and consumption rather than production; emphasise the household perspective; consider income and consumption jointly with wealth; give more prominence to the distribution of income, consumption and wealth; and

https://doi.org/10.1515/9783110735833-008

broaden income measures to non-market activities. The OECD then developed a Framework for Measuring Well-Being and Progress, built around three components: current well-being; inequalities in well-being outcomes; and resources for future well-being.

The key dimensions in the Framework for current well-being are: income and wealth; work and job quality; housing; health; knowledge and skills; environment quality; subjective well-being; safety; work-life balance; social connections; and civil engagement. The key dimensions of the resources for future well-being are: natural capital; economic capital; human capital; and social capital. The Statistics and Data Directorate has taken on the challenging task of developing ways of measuring these dimensions for the Better Life Initiative and to produce the regular *How's Life?* reports. These measures are now aligned with the Sustainable Development Goals (SDG) developed by the United Nations in 2015, and the OECD has developed an SDG Pathfinder allowing access to content on SDGs from six international organisations.

Growing Unequal?

While the increased emphasis on inequality really commenced in 2011, and was given impetus by the aftermath of the GFC, particularly after September 2008, the outputs on inequality coincided with the crisis and had begun before the GFC really bit. In this sense, the GFC underscored the need for the work on inequality, rather than the initial critique of GDP. In October 2008, the OECD published a report, *Growing Unequal? Income Distribution and Poverty in OECD Countries,* in response to public perceptions that inequality had increased substantially under globalisation over the preceding two decades.

Growing Unequal? brought together for the first time analyses of the distribution of income and poverty as of the mid-2000s in all OECD Member countries, with data for about two-thirds of them reported for the 20 years from the mid-1980s. The report provided StatLinks – URLs linking tables and graphs in the book to the spreadsheets containing the data.

The data indicated a general increase in income inequality over the period in question, but different from what was typically suggested. While the analysis found some interesting changes, such as decreasing pensioner poverty but increasing child poverty, *Growing Unequal?* reported that there had been an effectively unnoticeable increase of only 2 points on the Gini index of inequality over the 20 years of the analysis across the 30 member countries. There had been more movement in Mexico, which regularly registers as the one of the most, if not the most, unequal OECD Member and is much more unequal than the OECD average.

Several interviewees identified this initiative as a personal priority of Secretary-General Gurría and his Chief of Staff, Gabriela Ramos, and it may well be that this perspective was driven by their personal backgrounds in a country that was both more unequal than other members, and suffered from a much lower GDP per capita than most Members. (Mexico's GDP per capita performance has long been volatile, and declined by more than 20 percent during the GFC). Gurría had, for example, in a 1999 article in the *OECD Observer*, stressed that the OECD needed to aim at social well-being, not only economic growth, in order to ensure social cohesion, a view only strengthened by the impact of the GFC.

The analysis was very much focused on questions of distributive justice, rather than GDP per capita – perhaps because for most OECD Members, relative rather than absolute poverty was the issue. As is often said, changes in relative positions are painful – and therefore politically significant. The emergence of the 'Occupy' movement in 2011 and the publication of French economist Thomas Piketty's influential book *Capital in the Twenty-first Century* in 2014 gave further impetus to this work. Piketty's earlier work on inequality (such as his 2001 book *Les hauts revenus en France au XXᵉ siècle: Inégalités et redistributions, 1902–1998*) appears to have been very influential in the overall development of a focus on inequality in the OECD, and he was a frequent invitee at OECD events on the subject, presenting a seminar at the OECD on 'Rising Inequalities' in October 2013). Piketty attached considerable importance to distributive justice and inequality, rather than on the traditional reliance (inherent in the OECD's long-standing commitment to maximising sustainable growth) that economic growth will improve the lot of the poor – embodied in the aphorism that 'a rising tide lifts all boats'.

While GDP and especially GDP per capita improved in some Member countries after the GFC, growth was sluggish in many others and so a focus on distribution was perhaps understandable. Nevertheless, the focus has moved away from the fact that current generations are considerably better off than those of the past, regardless of relativities. There is a danger that the OECD might be accused of having lost sight of the importance of improvement in measures of absolute welfare and the benefits of addressing absolute poverty. This criticism was echoed by economic journalist Clive Crook, who remarked of Piketty's *Capital in the 21st Century* that it invites readers to believe not just that inequality is important, but that nothing else matters.

The OECD's increased focus on inequalities, which began with the 2008 report on Growing Unequal, was followed up in subsequent years with additional analyses and reports including: Divided We Stand (2011), In It Together (2015), A Broken Social Elevator? How to Promote Social Mobility (2018) and Under Pressure: The Squeezed Middle Class (2019).

The Framework for Policy Action on Inclusive Growth

In May 2018, the OECD launched a report for the Ministerial Council Meeting (MCM), *Opportunities for All: OECD Framework for Policy Action on Inclusive Growth*, showing that, while some countries were making progress in remedying inequalities, greater effort was needed because opportunities were worsening for low-income groups. The report therefore called for an 'urgent and concerted effort' on the part of governments to drive more inclusive, sustainable economic growth that would benefit all in society.

Gabriela Ramos, OECD Chief of Staff, Sherpa to the G20 and Leader of the Inclusive Growth Initiative, in her Foreword to *Opportunities for All,* drew attention to evidence the OECD had gathered in the previous decade that pointed to increased inequalities of income and opportunities in many countries. Specifically, she noted that the top 20 percent of the income distribution earned nine times more on average than the bottom 20 percent, and that the distribution of wealth was even more unequal, with the top 20 percent holding half, and the bottom 40 percent only 3 percent.

The transformative effects of globalisation, digitalisation, demographics and climate change on economies and societies were seen in *Opportunities for All* as providing new occasions for growth, but also creating risks of rising inequalities. The report saw that reducing inequalities by providing greater opportunities for all to contribute and succeed was a means of making growth beneficial for all, and at the same time building strong foundations for future prosperity. Considering equality in the initial formulation of growth policies was seen as preferable to trying to correct for inequalities later through redistribution measures.

To help countries assess their progress in achieving more inclusive growth, the OECD developed a 'dashboard' of indicators on issues such as income, growth, employment, education, environment and governance to assist countries and their people monitor progress toward inclusive growth goals. The Organisation also developed a new Policy Framework, placing emphasis on ensuring low-income groups had access to services so that they would be able to contribute to increases in productivity, growth and well-being. The analysis had demonstrated that policies improving the lot of the poorest in society resulted in gains in prosperity and well-being for everyone.

The concern of the new Framework was that social background continued to determine the life chances of people in many OECD countries, considered to be the more affluent in the world. Children in low-income families were more likely to suffer housing deficiencies, and were unlikely to have a chance of pursuing a career in high-skill occupations such as science. In many countries, the OECD's Programme for International Student Assessment (PISA) survey showed that children from poorer backgrounds at the age of 15 lagged better off children in academic performance by a year. A key element to the report was that it demonstrated how the pernicious effects of the intersection of factors in different policy areas affected well-being, with social mobility hampered by, for example, limited access to quality healthcare services, education and transport services for low-income groups and people living in poorer regions.

The chapter headings of the analysis underpinning the 'Framework for Policy Action on Inclusive Growth' provide a sense of its theme: Sustain growth that benefits all; Support business dynamism and inclusive labour markets; Invest in people and places left behind, providing equal opportunities; and Build efficient and responsive governments.

The OECD recommended in the Framework that countries take advantage of the return to growth of the global economy to adopt more ambitious structural reforms prioritising equity considerations. The Organisation argued that any short-term costs from reforms could be lower and shorter-lived when demand and job creation were stronger. The Framework recommended actions in three key areas:

- Investing in people and places 'left behind', particularly children at risk, through: targeted quality childcare, early education and life-long learning; access to quality healthcare services, education, justice, housing and infrastructures; and optimal natural resource management for sustainable growth.
- Supporting 'business dynamism' and inclusive labour markets through: broad-based innovation, with fast and deep technology diffusion; strong competition and vibrant entrepreneurship; access to good quality jobs, especially for women and under-represented groups; and more efforts to help people adapt to the future of work.
- Building efficient and responsive governments through: aligned policy packages across the whole-of-government; putting equity at the centre of the design of policies; and involving citizens in policy-making while strengthening integrity, accountability and international coordination.

The Framework built on a number of OECD projects and strategies, such as the Productivity-Inclusiveness Nexus, the Jobs Strategy currently under development, the Skills Strategy, Innovation Strategy, Going for Growth Strategy, Going Digital project and Green Growth Strategy. The OECD intends to undertake country-specific studies on Inclusive Growth to assist governments put in place a roadmap to grow more inclusively.

WISE Developments

In November 2020, the OECD established a centre that would that would bring together the agendas of well-being, inequalities, inclusion and sustainability that had been introduced over time as horizontal concerns throughout the Organisation, as it moved away from a narrower concern with economic performance measured by GDP, with the foundational aim of the Organisation being to maximise sustainable economic growth.

The Centre on Well-being, Inclusion, Sustainability and Equal Opportunity (WISE), was seen to be central to the OECD's response and recovery strategies in the face of the recession and uncertainty arising from the COVID-19 pandemic. The WISE mission is to strengthen the measurement of well-being, inequalities, inclusion and sustainability; and to develop better understanding of the impact of policies and business actions on both people's lives today, and on the sustainability of well-being over the longer term at the beginning of a 'decade of action' for the Sustainable Development Goals.

WISE was established in the belief that the COVID-19 pandemic had made it all the more important to understand people's perceptions and attitudes, because people's willingness to support policy was believed to be shaped, at least in part, by their perception of where they stood in their society and of what their prospects were. The aim was to 'get people and governments on the same page', and WISE introduced tools to serve this aim, such as well-being country reviews and the online tool *Compare Your Income*. This allows users to compare their household's income with the rest of the population and ascertain how many households are better or worse off than theirs, and see how their ideal world compares.

WISE incorporates a recognition that social inequality is very often rooted in early-life disadvantage, and that a disadvantaged childhood often leads to a disadvantaged adulthood, and thus limits social mobility. WISE therefore has also paid particular attention to child well-being outcomes and, from 2020, the impact of the COVID-19 pandemic on current inequalities. WISE seeks to emphasise the importance of equality of opportunity for all children, and the need to improve their life chances as well as those of future generations. It has established a *Child Well-Being Data Portal* to monitor child well-being inequalities, and sought to supplement the available data with policies that can protect children and enhance child well-being in post COVID-19.

In regards to sustainability, WISE is attempting to combine Inclusive Growth with Green Growth, reflecting a vision that Inclusive Growth also requires helping societies and economies transition to a green future. It has published a report setting this out: Inequalities-Environment Nexus: Towards a People-Centred Green Transition. Through this, WISE is attempting to set out inclusive and green policies, to consider the main challenges to such progress, and to identify solutions which countries might adopt in order to achieve a 'fair and green' transition as they recover from COVID-19.

WISE has also worked to support a partnership with business called Business for Inclusive Growth (B4IG) – launched under the G7 French Presidency in 2019 – to work with businesses throughout value chains to create a post COVID-19 recovery and a resilient future. B4IG is a partnership between the OECD and a global coalition of companies rather than business associations, led by their CEOs, designed to fight against inequalities of income and opportunities. Its rationale is that an increasing number of people in all societies are being left behind and not benefitting from the wealth created by globalisation and the technological revolution. The issues were seen as even more urgent in the light of the COVID-19 pandemic, with the fight against inequality considered more necessary than ever. B4IG states that it is united in helping to build stronger, more inclusive business models. The OECD is a Strategic Partner of B4IG, and supports it by coordinating with governments and leveraging its data, analysis, and global standards. Secretary-General Angel Gurría is Co-Chair of the B4IG Board, together with Emmanuel Faber, until recently Chairman and CEO of Danone. It is hosted by the OECD.

The companies that are members of B4IG pledge to play their part in advancing the G7 agenda to strengthen equality of opportunity; reduce territorial inequalities; promote diversity and inclusion; and reduce gender inequality. They further pledge to support a new model of growth by focusing actions around three key pillars 'fundamental to inclusive business': advancing human rights in direct operations and supply chains; building inclusive workplaces; and strengthening inclusion in company value chains and business ecosystems.

B4IG has enjoyed some limited success in recruiting corporations, with 40 firms joining. The membership is heavily slanted to those headquartered in the European Union, with only seven headquartered in the US and one in Japan, with three in the United Kingdom. Three members (Panera Bread, Pret-à-Manger, and Keurig Dr Pepper) trade in the US or UK, but are in fact subsidiaries of the German-owned conglomerate JAB Holding Company, which is also a member of B4IG and is headquartered in Luxembourg. Most of the members are large corporations trading transnationally, but they also include YLVA, which is owned by the Student Union of the University of Helsinki.

Several members have had recent challenges with what might be called broadly 'corporate social responsibility', such as Goldman Sachs and JP Morgan, which were central to the problems that caused the GFC. Johnson & Johnson, for example, has taken blows to its corporate image in various law suits, although this is a company with a long record with a concern for social justice.

The location of JAB in the tax haven of Luxembourg points to both a weakness of the group, but also an area where the scheme might lead to an improvement in corporate conduct. Another member, Accenture, is headquartered in Ireland, having moved there from Bermuda in 2010, and reportedly paid only 3.5 percent in tax in 2012. By committing to the B4IG Pledge, these companies are making a very public commitment to improve their corporate conduct and failure to do so will lead to increased pressure on them to respect their engagements.

Education and Skills

The work on inequality suggested that the labour market should be the first place to act, because better-educated, higher-earning workers have reaped higher gains while those with lower skills have been left behind. This and the OECD's increasing alignment with SDGs saw PISA becoming the metric for the quality of education in SDG Goal 4. Further, PISA expanded its scope to developing countries, broadened the assessment to include new competencies, including social competencies; and supplemented its assessments with work on curriculum design and teaching. PISA is limited to students in school, while the Programme for the International Assessment of Adult Competencies (PIAAC) created in 2011–2012, assesses and analyses adult skills. Conducted in over 40 countries/economies, it measures the key cognitive and workplace skills needed for individuals to participate in society and for economies to prosper.

Within the context of SDG Goal 4, the OECD's Education Policy Committee launched the 'Future of Education and Skills 2030' project in 2015, to help countries prepare their education systems for the longer-term future. The project has two phases. The first phase (2015–2019) focused on 'what' questions: what kinds of competencies (knowledge, skills, attitudes and values) students need to shape the future for better lives and for individual and societal well-being. The second phase (from 2019), focuses on 'how': how to design learning environments that can nurture such competencies, in other words how to implement curricula effectively. The OECD worked globally with policymakers, researchers, school leaders, teachers, students and social partners from 2016 to 2018 to develop a shared vision of education and a learning framework that sets out the types of competencies today's students need for the future.

The project's initial focus was on secondary education, but it recognises the importance of all levels of education and formal and informal education and lifelong learning. The OECD sees the project's principles as being applicable to all levels of learning, and its framework as able to serve as a common language to build a shared understanding that every learner, regardless of age or background, can fulfil their potential, and participate in and shape a future that improves the well-being of individuals, communities and the planet.

The project began by revising the OECD 'Definition and Selection of Competencies: Theoretical and Conceptual Foundations' (DeSeCo) project developed between 1997 and 2003 with the aim of providing theoretical and conceptual foundations to identify the key competencies needed for a successful life and a well-functioning society. The OECD 'Learning Framework 2030' is adventurous, incorporating new concepts not yet fully researched, and aiming to increase its relevance to policy makers by linking the framework to curriculum design issues. The Learning Framework uses the metaphor of the 'learning compass' to demonstrate the types of competencies students need in order to 'navigate' towards the future. The Learning Compass 2030 has seven elements:

1. Core foundations that are prerequisites for further learning across the entire curriculum.
2. Three 'transformative competencies' that students need for a better future: creating new value, reconciling tensions and dilemmas, and taking responsibility.

3. Student agency/co-agency. Student agency is defined as the belief that students have the will and the ability to positively influence their own lives and the world around them.
4. Knowledge, including theoretical concepts and ideas and practical understanding based on experience of having performed certain tasks. The project recognises four different types of knowledge: disciplinary, interdisciplinary, epistemic and procedural.
5. Skills, or the ability to carry out processes and use knowledge in a responsible way to achieve a goal. The Compass distinguishes three different types of skills: cognitive and metacognitive; social and emotional; and practical and physical.
6. Attitudes and values that influence one's choices, judgements, behaviours and actions on the path towards individual, societal and environmental well-being to strengthen and renew trust in institutions and among communities.
7. Anticipation-Action-Reflection cycle – an iterative learning process whereby learners continuously improve their thinking and act intentionally and responsibly.

This project supplements PIAAC.

The adoption of the SDGs enhanced the value of the PISA results and they are now being used by the UN system as a major source of data for monitoring progress towards the SDGs. The expanded concern for inequality has also encouraged the development of further instruments, such as PISA for Development, in which a modified PISA has been extended to less-developed countries, and an International Early Learning and Child Well-being Study (IELS), dubbed 'Baby PISA', which has allowed the OECD to expand its education activities well beyond its traditional scope.

Conclusion

The OECD has leapt boldly to reinterpret its constitutional requirement, embedded in its Convention, of maximising sustainable economic growth. For most of its history, that has meant a focus on increasing GDP, but this measure has long been questioned as the sole basis for assessing human welfare. The reason for this focus was well enough known: other aspects of welfare were notoriously difficult to measure. The OECD has not only led the world in attempting to overcome this difficulty by focusing on well-being and inclusion and developing statistical techniques to measure them, it has also sought to develop policies in education and skills development that will improve well-being and reduce inequality in future.

This is a brave step, and its success will be known only with time. As a Danish proverb (frequently misattributed) goes: 'It is difficult to make predictions, especially about the future.' It must be said, however, that the skills project seeks to build individuals resilient enough to adapt to whatever the future might bring.

9 Innovation and the Digital Economy

While the OECD's work on innmovation goes back to the 1960s, the work accelerated, albeit slowly, in the early 2000s as governments came increasingly to realise
the importance of innovation for driving economic growth. Work on the issue dramatically expanded after 2009 as governments faced the increasing policy challenges of innovation in the ICT sector and, most of all, the impact of digitalisation
on innovation and the growth of the digital economy. While work on the digital
economy began at least as early as 1985, in the last decade it has expanded rapidly.
This chapter outlines the major developments of the OECD's work on innovation
and the digital economy, work that has been opened up to participation by an increasing number of actors from the public and private sectors in Member and non-
member countries.

The Development of Work on Innovation at the OECD: 1992–2010

Interest at the OECD in innovation and the role it played in economic development
goes back at least to the Organisation's 'Gaps in Technology' report, 1968–1970, that
arose from concern in the 1960s about a growing 'technological gap' between the US
and other OECD countries, especially the seeming failure of university research to become applied in the economy, that is, a failure to innovate and stimulate growth
and productivity.

Policy interest in innovation grew rapidly in the 1980s and 1990s, including at
the OECD, where a number of Directorates became involved in work on the importance of innovation for economic growth, notably the Committee for Scientific and
Technological Policy (CSTP) and its Working Party on Innovation and Technology
Policy (TIP) and National Experts on Science and Technology Indicators (NESTI),
the Committee on Industry, Innovation and Entrepreneurship (CIIE), and the Centre
for Educational Research and Innovation (CERI), followed later by the Committee
for Information, Computer and Communications Policy.

The 1990s saw the establishment of the OECD's Technology Economy Programme
(TEP), which ran between 1992 and 1994 and brought in a range of international researchers to discuss innovation and growth, the innovation research agenda, indicator
needs (to do with human resources as well as innovation) and their policy implications. Most importantly, Keith Smith and Mikael Akeblom, working at the Finnish
Statistical Office, wrote the first draft of the 'Oslo Manual, or Proposed Guidelines
for Collecting and Interpreting Technological Innovation Data', as approved by NESTI
in 1992.

The Oslo Manual was a set of guidelines for collecting and interpreting data on
technological innovation, intended to be a basis for more coherent future surveys,

https://doi.org/10.1515/9783110735833-009

that focused on product and process innovation in manufacturing industries. The Manual proved popular and has since been updated on several occasions in co-operation with Eurostat, providing a set of guidelines for measuring innovation. It was followed by a series of largely national innovation surveys, such as those on Canada, Australia and the European Union. These surveys showed that it was possible to develop and collect data on complex and differentiated innovation phenomena that enabled valuable, cross-national studies and advice for the rapidly developing national innovation policies of OECD members.

The second, 1997 edition of the Manual included guidelines for measuring innovation in service industries. While primarily focused on technological innovation, the measurement of 'non-technological' innovation received increasing attention. The 2005, third edition again expanded the innovation measurement framework and also included service, organisational and marketing innovation, and the challenges associated with measuring innovation in developing countries. The fourth edition was published in 2018, with a focus on innovation and digitalisation, by which time its reputation was firmly established, as demonstrated by its influence on the 2016 Group of Twenty (G20) Innovation Action Plan, endorsed by G20 Leaders in Hangzhou.

An increasing range of separate innovation projects were developed at the OECD from the late 1990s into the 2000s. The 1999 'Managing National Innovation Systems' for example, promoted by the Deputy Director of STI, Bengt Ake Lundvall, examined the role and impact of national systems of innovation and the management challenges they represented. Linked to the national innovation system concept was the 2001 OECD report 'Innovative Clusters: Drivers of National Innovation Systems', expanding on the notion of innovation clusters, networks of interdependent firms, knowledge-producing institutions and bridging institutions linked in a production chain creating added value. Moreover, the 1998 'OECD Jobs Strategy: Technology, Productivity and Job Creation', showed how work practices based on innovation, advanced skills, organisational flexibility and trust, were often linked to higher labour productivity, higher sales, positive employment performance and lower staff turnover.

The increased work on innovation paralleled its rise to prominence in economic policy making, including an increasing number of country studies. For example, the 2000 OECD report 'A New Economy? The changing role of innovation and information technology in growth', helped to demonstrate the relationship between technological progress, innovation and economic growth, with innovation and technological change becoming increasingly important for economic performance. A range of reports that focused on innovation in different industry sectors also demonstrated the importance of innovation for energy technology and pharmaceutical biotechnology. The reports also indicated the importance of public sector support for innovation and the impact of governance for innovation systems, all expanding the understanding of the role of innovation and how it should be taken into consideration in policy. In addition, there was important work on the determinants of innovation and its outcomes at the enterprise level, which were influential in the increasing adoption of innovation policies by Members and other states.

Two innovation projects stand out from the 2000s, the OECD Innovation Microdata project and, most importantly, the development of the OECD's first Innovation Strategy, a three-year project, published in 2010. The Microdata project was the first large-scale exploration of firm-level data from innovation surveys, involving research teams from a range of countries using similar methodologies to collect comparable statistics and develop new indicators. The project's two major reports, 'Innovation in Firms' (2009) and 'Measuring Innovation: A New Perspective' (2010), revealed a range of new modes of innovation and provided a better understanding of the diversity of innovation performance at the micro level, including the fact that innovation could and did take place without significant research and development. It also stimulated the expansion of OECD's work on microdata, including work on businesses, patents and innovation.

The increasing understanding of innovation that the OECD work enabled also led to the realisation that more co-ordinated, whole-of-government approaches were needed to strengthen members' innovation performance and policy. This realisation was driven home in the OECD's 2007 'Innovation and Growth, Rationale for an Innovation Strategy' paper and by the G8's 2007 request that the OECD support a new dialogue on innovation, via its Heiligendamm Dialogue Process Support Unit. The paper contained a detailed argument in support of a proposal for the development of an innovation strategy, similar in intent to the earlier Jobs Strategy, and was put to OECD Ministers at the 2007 Meeting of the OECD Council at Ministerial Level (MCM), where it was strongly endorsed. Further urgency was added to the project by the damaging impact of the 2008 global financial crisis (GFC), with increased and appropriate investment in innovation for long-term economic growth seen as a vital part of the recovery efforts. The project was further reinforced in the 2009 paper 'Policy Responses to the Economic Crisis: Investing in Innovation for Long Term Growth'.

The 2010 Innovation Strategy and associated publications were the product of a wide range of OECD Committees, as well as external advisors, designed to assist governments make better innovation policy, placing it as an important element of economic policy regarding growth. They summarised much of the existing work on innovation and its implications for policy and saw the establishment of a web-based innovation portal, later to become 'The Innovation Policy Platform'. In turn, the Platform developed into STIP Compass, a web portal that provides access to a database developed jointly by the OECD and European Commission, launched in 2018. It makes available both quantitative and qualitative data on national science, technology and innovation policies, collected on a continuous basis. It also allows member countries to update information on a continuous basis.

In the 2012 evaluation of the Committee for Science and Technology Policy (CSTP), the Strategy was judged to have significantly enhanced the visibility of the Committee's work and to have had a useful impact on policy development. However, it was also concluded that the Strategy and associated publications were of limited use as the breadth of their approach had reduced the depth of analysis and policy recommendations. Developments such as STI Compass have gone a long way to remedying that situation, providing an increasingly important research tool of direct and easily accessible use for policy makers and researchers.

Innovation 2010–2021

The last decade has seen further work on innovation at the OECD, driven by the continuing aftermath of the GFC and the debt crises in Europe, and the search for policy solutions to the problems being faced. In this section we look at the 2015 revision of the 2010 Innovation Strategy, the 2016 G20 Innovation Report (an OECD report for the G20 Science, Technology and Innovation Ministers' meeting that illustrated the increasing value and influence of OECD work on innovation), a data-driven examination of the impact of R&D tax incentives and direct funding, the OECD microBeRD project and, most importantly, an increasing focus on the role of innovation in a digital age.

The 2010 Innovation Strategy was one of the first of a new generation of OECD horizontal projects that benefited from resources from the central priority fund. It was generally well received. A synthesis report, 'The OECD Innovation Strategy: Getting a Head Start on Tomorrow' was complemented by a revamped suite of indicators in a companion report 'Measuring Innovation: A New Perspective' which for the first time directly compared direct expenditures on R&D with indirect expenditures associated with R&D tax incentives, revealing the important and growing role of tax. In his 2013 Strategic Orientations, the Secretary-General pointed to the need to revisit and update the Innovation Strategy, a view endorsed by the 2014 MCM. The 2015 version 'The Innovation Imperative: Contributing to Productivity Growth and Well-being' was, again, a horizontal project, involving 14 Directorates, covering areas such as green innovation, health innovation and public sector innovation, led by the CSTP and CIIE. It focused more on providing and justifying advice for government innovation policies, emphasising the need to:
- Strengthen investment in innovation and foster business dynamism
- Invest in, and shape, an efficient system of knowledge creation and diffusion
- Seize the benefits of the digital economy
- Foster talent and skills and optimise their use
- Improve the governance and implementation of policies for innovation

Moreover, the Report argued, priorities needed to be tailored to meet a range of possible, country-specific innovation policy agendas, with the Report providing examples of such agendas for high income countries; low to medium income countries;

resource-based economies; and small and emerging economies; as well for inclusiveness and green growth.

The OECD MicroBeRD project, carrying on the tradition of microdata studies established in the earlier, OECD Innovation Microdata project, further explored the question of the mix of policies to stimulate R&D. It also investigated whether tax incentives and direct funding were effective in stimulating additional R&D investment by businesses. The project provided new, largely survey-based evidence on the impact of R&D tax incentives and direct funding of business R&D, drawing on distributed cross-country and firm-level analyses undertaken as part of the first phase of the project over 2016–2019, with the second phase planned for 2020–2023, undertaken jointly by CIIE and CSTP, led by NESTI. The second phase investigates the impact of R&D on innovation outputs such as new products and services, and their broader economic outcomes on employment and productivity growth.

Among the major findings from the project were:
- Both R&D tax incentives and direct funding were effective in incentivising R&D investment by business, with one monetary unit (EUR) of either tax or direct support leading to approximately 1.4 units of business R&D.
- R&D tax incentives helped increase in R&D activity among existing R&D performers and entice firms to start or continue investing in R&D.
- R&D tax incentive is larger for firms that perform less R&D, such as smaller firms.
- The effect of R&D tax incentives on experimental development is about twice as large as the effect on basic and applied research, while the effect of direct funding on experimental development is half as large as the effect on basic and applied research.
- Firm-level results demonstrated wide variations in the impact of R&D tax incentives and direct funding across countries.

The data derived from the project also played an important part in the development and use of the OECD's R&D Tax Incentives Database that provides policymakers and researchers with data on the use and impact of R&D tax incentives across a range of economies.

Innovation and Digitalisation

The years between 2010 and 2021 have seen an explosion of work on innovation and digitalisation across the OECD, coming together under the OECD's Going Digital Initiative. This work was stimulated, in part, by earlier publications such as the 'Merger Review in Emerging High innovation Markets' (2002), 'Competition, Patents and Innovation' (2006 and 2009) and notably by two horizontal projects,

'Supporting Investment in Knowledge Capital, Growth and Innovation' (2013), and 'Data Driven Innovation' (2015).

The work was given added impetus by the 2016 OECD Ministerial Cancun Declaration on the Digital Economy, 'Stimulating Digital Innovation across the Economy', which noted that Ministers would 'Stimulate digital innovation and creativity to spur growth and address global social issues through coordinated policies that promote investment in digital technologies and knowledge-based capital, encourage availability and use of data, including open public sector data, foster entrepreneurship and the development of small and medium enterprises, and support the continued transformation of all economic sectors, including public services'.

The Declaration helped spur the OECD's Going Digital initiative, launched in January 2017 as 'Going Digital: Making the Transformation Work for Growth and Well-being' which soon became known as the Going Digital project, material from which was used for the 2017 G20 Innovation Report prepared by the OECD. Going Digital aimed to help policymakers better understand the digital transformation taking place and create appropriate policy responses.

Among the several projects under the Going Digital umbrella was the Working Party on Innovation and Technology Policy's (TIP) innovation and digitalisation project, initiated in 2016, and the OECD Digital Economy paper 'Stimulating Digital Innovation for Growth and Inclusiveness: The Role of Policies for the Successful Diffusion of ICT', also published in 2016. The TIP project culminated in a final publication 'Digital Innovation: Seizing Policy Opportunities', a synthesis of the main findings, which explored the effects that digital innovation was having on innovation policies. It also identified policy implications from the project, based on its reviews of changing innovation dynamics across industry sectors and different actors, with a focus on SMEs, start-ups and research institutions, with a particular focus on new forms of collaboration. The most significant outputs of Phase I of the Going Digital projects are noted in the following section.

The OECD and the Digital Economy

The OECD at an early stage developed guidance to facilitate electronic commerce, beginning with a Declaration from the Ottawa Ministerial Conference, 'A Borderless World: Realising the Potential of Global Electronic Commerce' in December 1998. Then, on 9 December 1999, the Council approved Guidelines for Consumer Protection in the Context of Electronic Commerce (updated in 2016). These were intended to ensure a level of protection for consumers shopping online, thus minimising uncertainties that might be associated with e-commerce for both buyers and sellers. The Guidelines reflect the existing legal protections available to more conventional consumers. The Guidelines were developed after 18 months of consultations with representatives of Member governments as well as business and consumer interests, and assisted governments and groups representing these interests to develop consumer protection measures that do not amount to barriers to trade.

The Guidelines stress the need for co-operation among governments, businesses and consumers, to encourage: fair business, advertising and marketing practices; clear information about an online business's identity, the goods or services it offers and the terms and conditions of any transaction; a transparent process for the confirmation of transactions; secure payment mechanisms; fair, timely and affordable dispute resolution and redress; privacy protection; and consumer and business education.

The OECD in fact had begun to lay the basis for the global digital economy with the adoption of OECD Guidelines on the Protection of Privacy and Transborder Flows of Personal Data Privacy in 1980 and then, in 1985, with the adoption of the OECD Declaration on Transborder Data Flows, designed to promote access to transborder data and services, and avoid unjustified barriers to data exchange. It also sought transparency in related regulations and policies; common approaches; and to consider the impact of actions on other countries. That initiative coincided with the first of a series of OECD Digital Economy Papers. Many of the early papers in this series focused on telecommunications and trade in digital services, but by the late 1990s began to focus on e-commerce, with 'Payments for Goods and Services on the Information Superhighway' (1996), 'Measuring Electronic Commerce' (1997), and 'Electronic Commerce' (1997). Such work increasingly continued to lay down the standards to facilitate e-commerce with papers such as 'Online Payment Systems for E-commerce' (2006). At the time of writing, 307 Digital Economy Papers have been published.

The OECD has also developed a considerable number of legal instruments in the area, culminating in the 23 June Cancún Declaration at the 2016 Ministerial Meeting of the Committee on Digital Economy Policy. The Organisation also took action to address the problem of spam, with the adoption by Council on 13 April 2006 of the OECD Recommendation on Cross-Border Co-operation in the Enforcement of Laws against Spam. This was developed by a Task Force supported by voluntary financial contributions from Australia, the Czech Republic, Italy, and Norway.

The Next Production Revolution

An important element of the Going Digital project has been work on what has become more broadly known as the Fourth Industrial Revolution – or, in the OECD, the Next Production Revolution. This has involved examining the opportunities and challenges of digital technologies such as 'the Internet of Things', industrial biotechnology, 3D printing, new materials and nanotechnology that are thought to have far-reaching consequences for productivity, skills, income distribution, well-being, and the environment.

This echoes the focus of the World Economic Forum (WEF) on the Fourth Industrial Revolution, which was given currency by its executive chairman, Klaus Schwab, in an essay published in Foreign Affairs in December 2015, 'Mastering the Fourth Industrial Revolution', but had its origins in an earlier strategy developed by the German government in 2011 as 'Industrie 4.0' (often shortened to 'I4.0' or simply 'I4') promoting the computerisation of manufacturing. This was also the theme of the 2016 WEF Annual Meeting in Davos, reflecting a close relationship between the OECD under Secretary-General Gurría and the WEF, where Gurría serves as a member of the board of trustees. This mirroring was also seen with the adoption of the slogan 'Building Back Better' by the OECD as a response to the COVID-19 pandemic (and by the United Kingdom as well as the Biden presidential campaign) and also the focus on 'Inclusive Growth' by the WEF.

The OECD commenced work early in 2015 on a two-year project entitled 'Enabling the Next Production Revolution', supported by the Secretary-General's Central Priority Fund and voluntary contributions from the Australian and United Kingdom governments. The Committee on Industry, Innovation and Entrepreneurship published an issues paper 'Enabling the Next Production Revolution' in March 2015 that had been prepared as a background document for the conference 'Shaping the Strategy for Tomorrow's Production' organised by the Danish Production Council in Copenhagen on 27 February 2015. Support from Norway allowed the scope to be widened. Moreover, in November 2016, the Swedish Ministry for Enterprise and Innovation and its national innovation agency, Vinnova, hosted a major conference on the themes of the project, 'Smart Industry: Enabling the Next Production Revolution'. The result was a report, 'The Next Production Revolution: Implications for Governments and Business', launched under the Italian Presidency of the G7, for which the Organisation worked closely with China during its G20 Presidency, and which (in its Preface) explicitly referenced 'the fourth industrial revolution'.

As with the work on artificial intelligence (AI) discussed below, the horizontal nature of work on the next production revolution meant it cut across the 'silos' of the Directorates and Committees. The chapters of 'The Next Production Revolution' were therefore discussed and declassified by several committees, including: the Committee for Scientific and Technological Policy (which had oversight responsibility for the project); the Committee for Industry, Innovation and Entrepreneurship; the Committee for Digital Economy Policy; and the Environment Policy Committee. The project was led within the Secretariat by the Directorate for Science, Technology and Innovation (STI). An interim report was then discussed by the Executive Committee and Council and was presented at the Ministerial Council Meeting in June 2016.

Issues relating to digital technologies raised in this report, with fresh data, were then examined during 2017 and 2018, in the project Going Digital: Making the Transformation Work for Growth and Well-being.

Artificial Intelligence

The work on the digital economy was adeptly extended to the important emerging issues surrounding artificial intelligence (AI). In 2016, the Committee on Digital Economy Policy discussed the need for a Recommendation on AI principles, which followed an annex on 'Ethical Guidelines for AI R&D' issued by the G7 Digital Ministerial in Takamatsu, Japan. In May 2018, an expert group was established to develop principles that could be adopted in 2019. The Expert Group grew particularly out of an October 2017 conference, 'AI: Intelligent Machines, Smart Policies', where a consensus emerged that the far-reaching changes arising from AI systems provided opportunities to improve the public, economic and social sectors. The conference focused on ways AI could make business more productive, improve government efficiency, and address pressing problems. The expert group consisted of representatives of Member states, experts from Members, invited experts, and experts nominated by the trade union and business advisory Committees TUAC and BIAC – the latter including representatives of Microsoft, Google, Facebook and IBM. Nineteen countries were represented on the AI expert group, joined by representatives from the European Commission, business and labour groups, and outside groups like the Institute of Electrical and Electronics Engineers, MIT, Harvard's Berkman Klein Center, and the French Institute for Research in Computer Science and Automation.

The work on the digital economy developed in 2017 into the Going Digital project, examining how the digital transformation affects policy-making across a wide spectrum of policy areas: competition; consumer policy; digital economy policy (privacy, security, infrastructure, economic impact); science, technology and innovation; industry and entrepreneurship; insurance and private pensions; financial markets; fiscal affairs and taxation; statistics; economic policy (monetary, fiscal and structural); education and skills; employment and social affairs; public governance; and trade. The Going Digital project aims to bring about stronger and more inclusive growth from the digital revolution by building a coherent and comprehensive policy approach.

While the Going Digital project is led and coordinated by the Committee on Digital Economic Policy, it is a horizontal project that involves the following Committees:
- Competition Committee
- Committee on Consumer Policy
- Committee on Industry, Innovation and Entrepreneurship
- Insurance and Private Pensions Committee
- Committee on Financial Markets
- Committee on Fiscal Affairs
- Committee on Scientific and Technological Policy
- Committee on Statistics and Statistics Policy
- Economic Policy Committee

- Education Policy Committee
- Employment, Labour and Social Affairs Committee
- Public Governance Committee
- Trade Committee

It may draw on other Committees and bodies such as the International Transport Forum, the Health Committee, the Environment Policy Committee, the Committee for Agriculture, the Investment Committee, and the International Energy Agency.

The first phase of the project led to the Going Digital Summit in March 2019, with the release of two reports, 'Going Digital: Shaping Policies, Improving Lives' and 'Measuring the Digital Transformation: A Roadmap for the Future'. The second phase (2019–2020) had two dimensions: assist countries to implement an integrated policy approach to the digital transformation, particularly by the further development of the Going Digital Toolkit, which contains indicators, policy notes and innovative policy examples, and by means of country reviews; and address new opportunities and challenges by means of analysis of two 'frontier technologies' that given their general application would have a large impact on a range of public policies: artificial intelligence and Blockchain.

On 22 May 2019, during the Ministerial Council Meeting, OECD countries adopted a Recommendation on Artificial Intelligence (OECD/LEGAL/0449) containing a set of OECD Principles on Artificial Intelligence aimed at promoting AI that is innovative and trustworthy and that respects human rights and democratic values. These were the first signed up to by governments anywhere, and were opened for adherence by non-member countries, with Argentina, Brazil, Costa Rica, Malta, Peru, Romania and Ukraine among the first to do so, with further adherents welcomed. The Principles complement existing OECD standards in areas such as privacy, digital security risk management and responsible business conduct, and are intended to be practical and flexible enough to remain relevant over time in a fast-moving field. Very soon after their adoption, in June 2019, the G20 adopted a set of AI Principles that drew on the OECD Principles.

The Recommendation specified the following five principles for the responsible stewardship of trustworthy AI:
- AI should benefit people and the planet by driving inclusive growth, sustainable development and well-being.
- AI systems should be designed in a way that respects the rule of law, human rights, democratic values and diversity, and they should include appropriate safeguards – for example, enabling human intervention where necessary – to ensure a fair and just society.
- There should be transparency and responsible disclosure around AI systems to ensure that people understand AI-based outcomes and can challenge them.

- AI systems must function in a robust, secure and safe way throughout their life cycles and potential risks should be continually assessed and managed.
- Organisations and individuals developing, deploying or operating AI systems should be held accountable for their proper functioning in line with the above `principles.

One initiative arising from the Recommendation on Artificial Intelligence was the development of metrics to measure AI research, development and deployment and to develop an evidence base to assess progress in the implementation of the Recommendation. To this end, in February 2020 the OECD launched the OECD AI Policy Observatory to serve as a source of evidence and guidance on AI metrics, policies and practices and to assist in the implementation of the Principles and provide a hub to facilitate dialogue and sharing of best practice on AI policies. The OECD convoked a multi-stakeholder expert advisory group (ONE AI) to provide technical expertise and develop tools and practical guidance for the implementation of the Principles. In June 2020, under the leadership of the French and Canadian Presidencies of the G7, the Global Partnership on AI (GPAI) was formed by 15 founding members. Its Secretariat is hosted by the OECD with a mission to achieve strong synergies between technical and policy work on AI.

In responding to the issues of the digital economy, the OECD has demonstrated an ability to react nimbly and proactively to emerging issues as – or arguably before – they arise, helped by the provision of strategic funds by the Secretary-General and Members. Work on the digital economy also demonstrates the OECD's well-established capacity to provide important inputs to the G20.

Conclusion

Work on innovation and the digital economy has both grown and become greatly more interconnected at the OECD over the last decade, mirroring a similar development in the advanced economies. It has been work strongly supported not only by Members, but by world leaders at the G7 and G20. It is also a domain in which the social dimensions of innovation and the digital economy have received increasing attention, part of the OECD's ongoing concern for inclusive growth and the desire to ensure that innovation and the digital economy do not further exacerbate growing inequality in society.

10 International Taxation

The OECD has a long involvement with tax policy. It developed a Model Double Taxation Convention in 1963, only two years after its formation, and revised it in 1977, facilitating international business by removing the threat that corporations and individuals would have to pay tax twice. The OECD model was subsequently used as the template for the development of a United Nations Model Double Taxation Convention between Developed and Developing Countries in 1980, and the development of bilateral 'East West' tax treaties during the Cold War, the first of these being concluded between the US and the USSR in 1973. This Model Tax Convention (MTC) has been updated regularly and has had a wide impact. It has been estimated that more than 3,000 bilateral tax treaties have been based on it.

Some tax practices are harmful, however, and an aggressive use of transfer pricing by multinationals to shift revenue between subsidiaries so that profits were taken in lower tax jurisdictions, was a problem. Tax competition grew between jurisdictions, with tax havens or low tax jurisdictions competing to attract business and thus revenue that would not otherwise accrue to them. In 1979, the OECD published its first report on *Transfer Pricing and Multinational Enterprises*. In 1995, the OECD developed guidelines to address this problem. These guidelines were updated in 1996, 2010, and most recently in 2017.

Concern over issues such as such harmful tax competition, or, more broadly, 'harmful tax practices' (HTP) was one of the key elements that led to the 'Base Erosion and Profit Shifting' (BEPS) Project launched in 2012 by the G20 and the OECD. Associated with this expansion in mission, there was a considerable expansion in staff in the OECD Secretariat. In 1972, when Jeffrey Owens joined the Secretariat of the OECD, the staff working on tax matters numbered three people, mostly engaged on double taxation treaties and tax statistics. By 2012, when Owens retired, a Centre for Tax Policy and Administration had been formed separate from the Directorate for Financial, Fiscal and Enterprise Affairs (by then, the Directorate for Financial and Enterprise Affairs). The Centre for Tax Policy and Tax Administration (CTPA) then had a staff of more than 100, from 25 countries, including staff from non-member countries. There are now around 200.

This chapter first traces the early work on tax in the OECD, noting the impediment to effective progress constituted by the presence among its membership of countries operating tax havens. It details the evolution from the Harmful Taxation Competition Initiative to the Base Erosion and Profit Shifting Project, together with the growth in importance of intellectual property, before describing the success in the past decade, which has enhanced the reputation of the OECD – both on tax policy and beyond.

https://doi.org/10.1515/9783110735833-010

From Double Taxation to the Harmful Taxation Competition Initiative

The prevalence of tax avoidance and evasion eventually led to the establishment within the Committee on Fiscal Affairs (CFA) of Working Party No.8 on Tax Avoidance and Evasion, which first met in March 1977. The CFA and its Working Parties provided both a point of contact where information could be sought from other Member Countries and a means of monitoring tax developments, not just in Member countries but in other international arenas.

Work in the OECD to address the problem of tax havens has been bedevilled by the fact that some were operated by Members of the Organisation, which both made agreement on actions difficult and weakened its moral authority as an exemplar. This was apparent with early work in cooperation with the Council of Europe. The negotiation draft Multilateral Convention on Cooperation Between the Council of Europe and the OECD Concerning Mutual Assistance in Tax Matters took some time, especially because some Members took exception to the prospect of being named as a tax haven. The International Chamber of Commerce and the Business and Industry Advisory Committee were also critical of the proposed Convention, and lobbying in Germany led to repeated German requests to delay the vote in the Council of Europe. When eventually put to the vote in April 1987, Germany voted against the text, joined by Switzerland and Luxembourg of the OECD and Liechtenstein of the Council of Europe. Having tax havens as Members of the OECD, including then the Netherlands and Ireland, was a constant drag on progress.

In 1996, on the initiative of the US, the then G8 requested the OECD to address the issue of harmful tax competition. At the 1996 Ministerial Council Meeting (MCM), the OECD established a work programme under the CFA leading to a report in April 1998, *Harmful Tax Competition: An Emerging Global Issue*, identifying two types of HTC: tax havens and preferential tax regimes (PTRs). There followed what was called the Harmful Tax Competition Initiative (HTCI). In parallel, to address the problem of bank secrecy, which facilitates tax evasion, it then published a report *Improving Access to Bank Information for Tax Purposes* in 2000.

An important aspect of addressing tax avoidance was the development of agreement of states to share financial information, including ownership and transactional information. The standard of transparency and exchange of information developed by the OECD was primarily contained in Article 26 of the OECD Model Tax Convention. The 2002 Model Agreement on Exchange of Information on Tax Matters, designed to facilitate exchange of information with tax havens, was limited to exchange of information on request. This was then expanded to include a system of automatic exchange of information in 2014.

The Global Forum on Taxation (the Global Forum) was established in 2000 as a way to engage with tax havens that had committed to implementing transparency and exchange of information standards. In 2009, the Global Forum was restructured to become the Global Forum on Transparency and Exchange of Information for Tax Purposes, and to allow all countries and jurisdictions to participate on an equal footing. Today it comprises 162 member jurisdictions plus the European Union and 19 regional and international organisations as observers.[1] Over the past decade EUR 107 billion of additional revenues (tax, interest, penalties) have been identified, bank deposits in international financial centres have fallen by USD 410 billion, 36 000 exchanges related to tax rulings have occurred between jurisdictions and close to 300 tax regimes have been reviewed. In 2019, countries automatically exchanged information on 84 million financial accounts worldwide, covering total assets of EUR 10 trillion.

The HTCI was widely regarded as having underachieved, although it did lay the foundations for the very successful Global Forum, and for the Forum on Harmful Tax Practices, which continues its work to this day as a key component of the BEPS project, discussed more fully below.

One emergent problem – exacerbated by increasing globalisation – is the growing importance of intellectual property and other intangibles, and the ease of transnational financial transactions that both resulted in increased opportunities for aggressive tax planning aimed at not being taxed anywhere ('double non-taxation'). For example, the physical cost of an iPhone is perhaps 10% of the retail price of the item, and the value of the IP can readily be captured in a jurisdiction where the tax regime is most favourable by locating the IP-owning subsidiary there. IP is more difficult to value and more difficult to track and control than say, transfer pricing with mineral resources, where there is a physical commodity and a market such as the London Metal Exchange with which to compare the value of transactions.

Information technology corporations, both software and hardware, such as Microsoft and Apple have used tax avoidance and transfer pricing devices to shift profits to low tax jurisdictions, although the issue is not simply confined to the technology sector. For example, Starbucks' UK subsidiary was paying patent fees to their US subsidiary and the Netherlands subsidiary (where corporation tax is lower than in the UK), while the Swiss subsidiary provided other 'miscellaneous services'. The Netherlands government granted a special tax rate to Starbucks' European headquarters, and the tax law of the Netherlands, alone in the EU, permitted companies to transfer royalties collected from other countries to tax havens without incurring taxes. The coffee beans

---

1 The African Development Bank, the African Tax Administration Forum, the African Union Commission, the Asian Development Bank, the Caribbean Community, the Cercle de Réflexion et d'Échange des Dirigeants des Administrations Fiscales, the Commonwealth Secretariat, the Council of Europe Development Bank, the European Bank for Reconstruction and Development, the European Investment Bank, the Financial Action Task Force, the Inter-American Center of Tax Administrations, the Inter-American Development Bank, the International Finance Corporation, the International Monetary Fund, the Intra-European Organisation of Tax Administrations, the United Nations, the World Bank Group and the World Customs Organisation.

used in the UK were purchased from the subsidiary in Switzerland, but never touched the ground there, although quality assurance was conducted (and paid for) there. Green coffee beans were bought from a Swiss subsidiary and then sold at a 20 percent mark-up to the roasting subsidiary in Amsterdam, which then sold the roasted beans to Starbucks outlets. In 2008, tax authorities in the Netherlands issued a new tax ruling for Starbucks, which resulted in the coffee roasting subsidiary sending large royalty payments to a company called Alki for use of a bean roasting recipe, practically eliminating the Dutch tax bill.

Intellectual property, in other words, is hard to tax. The Irish, French and German subsidiaries of Starbucks were also either owned by or indebted to the Dutch subsidiary, which charged them higher interest rates than the group paid to borrow. This 'thin capitalisation', using debt rather than equity and payment of higher than market rates for interest is another means of profit shifting.

The persistence of such practices was detracting from the revenue base of nations. When the Global Financial Crisis (GFC) struck in 2008, this loss of revenue took on a new urgency, and the support provided to financial institutions by governments to prevent their failure strengthened the moral case for action. This resulted in the BEPS project.

Base Erosion and Profit Shifting

The OECD has estimated that such practices, known as Base Erosion and Profit Shifting (or BEPS) cost countries up to $US 240bn in lost annual revenue, with developing countries worst affected because of their greater relative reliance on corporate tax revenue.

The global financial crisis of 2008/2009 provided both a need for and an opportunity to address the erosion of national tax bases. The response of governments to take on debt in order to provide stimulus meant the loss of revenue by governments took on new and urgent meaning. The response to the GFC provided the OECD with an opportunity to promote the tax avoidance work it had been pursuing, but which had lacked political support from leaders. Secretary-General Gurría and his staff, including Pascal Saint-Amans, then Head of the Global Forum Division of the Centre for Tax Policy and Administration, and now CTPA Director, undertook intensive and successful lobbying to get the issue on to the G20 agenda, demonstrating how quickly the OECD could move.

The GFC also increased the political pressure to take action because several of the banks and finance companies that had taken advantage of the existing system had been bailed out by governments – using public monies derived in large part from the tax revenues their avoidance strategies had eroded. The G20 was thus able to harness the resulting public ire in support of its endorsement of the OECD's tax work, which has grown substantially since that time.

The impetus given by the GFC led eventually to the development of BEPS, but it first encouraged the Organisation to rather boldly prepare and release what became known in the media as a 'black list' reporting on whether countries – including Members – were meeting the international standard on minimising tax avoidance.

On 2 April 2009, at the end of the G20 summit in London, the CTPA issued a Progress Report on the Jurisdictions Surveyed by the OECD Global Forum in Implementing the Internationally Agreed Tax Standard. That was the OECD's standard, developed in co-operation with non-OECD countries and which was endorsed by G20 Finance Ministers at their Berlin Meeting in 2004 and by the UN Committee of Experts on International Cooperation in Tax Matters at its October 2008 Meeting. It required exchange of information on request in all tax matters for the administration and enforcement of domestic tax law without regard to a domestic tax interest requirement or bank secrecy. It also provided for extensive safeguards to protect the confidentiality of the information exchanged.

The Progress Report on the implementation of the tax standard, identified: jurisdictions that had substantially implemented the standard; jurisdictions that had committed to but not yet implemented the standard, and tax havens that had committed to but not yet implemented the standard; and jurisdictions that had not committed to the standard. It was a bold move, given that some Member jurisdictions were named. (The 'grey list' of countries that had agreed to improve transparency standards but had not yet signed the necessary international accords included Luxembourg, Switzerland, Austria, Belgium, Singapore and Chile, as well as the Cayman Islands, Liechtenstein and Monaco). The publication of the list, under the authority of the Secretary-General, enhanced the reputation of the OECD, especially with the G20, as an organisation that had the capacity to deliver better outcomes, and this was to result in further referrals from the G20.

In 2012, the G20 asked the OECD to develop a BEPS Action Plan, which was approved at the 2013 G20 meeting. The Plan contained 15 Actions to address tax avoidance, improve coherence of international tax rules, and provide a more transparent global tax environment.

The range of measures adopted can be seen by surveying the titles of the Actions:
- Action 1: Address the Digital Economy
- Action 2: Hybrid mismatches
- Action 3: Controlled Foreign Companies (CFC) Rules
- Action 4: Interest Deductions
- Action 5: Harmful Tax Practices (*minimum standard*)
- Action 6: Treaty Abuse (*minimum standard*)
- Action 7: Permanent Establishment Status
- Actions 8–10: Transfer Pricing
- Action 11: BEPS Economic Analysis
- Action 12: Mandatory Disclosure Rules
- Action 13: Transfer Pricing Documentation (*minimum standard*)

- Action 14: Dispute Resolution (*minimum standard*)
- Action 15: Multilateral Instrument

This last Action addressed the legal and technical difficulties faced by the BEPS project in its aim to create a multilateral tax framework. The multilateral instrument, the Multilateral Convention to Implement Tax Treaty Related Measures to Prevent Base Erosion and Profit Shifting, was approved by the G20 and adopted on 24 November 2016 and came into force in July 2018.

The OECD/G20 Inclusive Framework on BEPS was established in 2016 to ensure a collective and effective implementation of the BEPS measures. To date, there are 139 countries and jurisdictions working on an equal footing. As noted above, among the 14 actions, four – Actions 5, 6, 13 and 14 – were adopted as 'minimum standards', core measures that countries committed to implement in a coordinated manner. As opposed to the other BEPS actions, ranging 'from common approaches' to 'best practices', the four minimum standards were agreed to tackle issues where no action by some countries would have resulted in negative spillovers on others. The NGO Tax Justice Network called the MLI a failure because of the opt-outs and watering-down of BEPS Actions, indicating it did not meet with total approval.

The OECD continued its efforts, releasing a policy note in January 2019, *Addressing the Tax Challenges of the Digitalisation of the Economy*, to develop new proposals to combat the BEPS activities of multinationals. The note was labelled by some commentators as 'BEPS 2.0'. In announcing the proposals, the OECD stated that they had the support of the US, China, Brazil and India. It was proposed that there should be a global system of taxation based on where a product was consumed or used, rather than where its IP was located. Predictably, the Irish media saw a threat to Ireland as the world's largest BEPS hub, as it had proportionately fewer consumers relative to business activity than most countries.

The OECD/G20 Inclusive Framework on BEPS then produced reports on blueprints for a 'Two Pillar' approach for the October 2020 G20 meeting of finance ministers. Pillar One would provide a new taxing right to allocate a percentage of residual profits of multinational companies to market jurisdictions. Pillar Two would provide for a global minimum tax to ensure multinational profits incur a minimum level of taxation, no matter how much tax planning is deployed. From February to October 2020, the Steering Groups and Working Parties of the Inclusive Framework conducted almost 70 days of mostly virtual meetings to advance the technical work on these proposals in the face of the COVID-10 pandemic. The two pillars have the potential to increase annual global corporate tax collections by up to $US 100bn. (The Inclusive Framework is intended to finalise this agreement by mid-2021).

The work on tax has been assisted through bilateral collaboration between the OECD and the European Commission, anchored in a Financial Framework Partnership Agreement, up for renewal in 2021. Under this Agreement, the two organisations implemented over 145 cooperation projects in three years, from responsible supply chains to investment and sustainable development. The collaboration on digital taxation is considered to have been of considerable value for enhancing global tax fairness.

After decades of setting standards in the area of tax treaties and transfer pricing, and fighting against double taxation, the OECD, assisted by the urgency of the GFC, produced significant efforts to limit the ability of major finance companies to facilitate multinational enterprises and high-net-worth individuals (HNWIs) subvert domestic tax systems and international tax agreements in ways that had significantly reduced the tax revenues available to governments. The bold move of naming transgressors, including Member jurisdictions, cemented the support of the G20, which moved from a meeting of finance ministers to one involving heads of government with the GFC, but lacked the research and analytical capability that the OECD could provide. With G20 support, the OECD has been able to progress its work on limiting the use of tax havens both by MNEs and HNWIs. This has been a substantial achievement, given that at least four of its Members themselves had strict bank secrecy rules.

Naming non-compliant OECD Members has helped establish the OECD's moral authority and its engagement with non-members, which has also significantly increased over time. OECD tax work was opened up to non-OECD countries from the early 2000s with some key G20 countries being invited as observers in the CFA, and then the creation of global fora for dialogue between OECD and non-OECD countries. The CFA was the first major Committee of the OECD to begin opening up and this accelerated after the success of the Organisation at the G20 2009 Leaders' summit, to the point that the OECD Inclusive Framework now has 139 members. The success of tax work has also been assisted because it has produced substantial benefits for developing countries as well as OECD Member countries, overcoming a longstanding perception that the OECD is a 'club of the rich'. The success has also resulted in the G20 engaging more deeply with the OECD on other issues.

However, involving more participants ran the risk of either lower quality outcomes or even failure to achieve meaningful outcomes. Success required as close to global coverage as possible, but more participants also bring problems. US diplomat George F. Kennan once observed that the unlikelihood of a negotiation reaching agreement grows by the square of the number of parties taking part. The OECD has overcome these challenges, and the bold decision by the Secretary-General to name transgressors not only secured the Organisation a place at the centre of global tax policy reform, but was also significant in gaining OECD a continuing relationship with the G-20.

The progress on global tax reform is a credit to the OECD, and especially the CTPA. The CTPA has sustained what is regarded as an energetic and effective staff with a strong sense of camaraderie. It is a well-established challenge that tax administrators are difficult to recruit and retain, meaning that public agencies often train them and give them experience before they are lured away by more attractive salaries in the tax minimisation sector, meaning agency staff are often engaged in a contest with those better trained (and at public expense). This seems to have been largely avoided in the CTPA, largely thanks to the leadership, first of Jeffrey Owens and then more lately of Pascal Saint-Amans. While staff recruitment has been difficult because of the salary differential, high staff retention has minimised this problem.

Conclusion

The path to a better global tax system has been long and difficult one. After the rather 'damp squib' of the HTCI, the recent progress reflects well on the organisation which, thanks largely to the policy entrepreneurship of Secretary-General Gurría and the skill of the CTPA, has seen the OECD become the pre-eminent international agency in the field. Additionally, the success on tax policy has helped enhance the reputation of the Organisation in other policy domains beyond the field of tax.

11 Systemic Thinking and Smart Data

The 2010s saw a considerable transformation of the work of the OECD and the infrastructure, physical as well as intellectual, that supports it. This can be clearly seen in the three developments examined in this chapter: New Approaches to Economic Challenges (NAEC), Strategic Foresight and Smart Data. NAEC is an ongoing attempt to develop new, more sophisticated understandings of socio-economic systems, to better support and, where appropriate, modify or overturn traditional assumptions and the economic and social policy analysis and recommendations built upon them. Strategic Foresight, along with NAEC, is a small unit based in the Office of the Secretary-General (OSG), under the supervision of the Chief of Staff, providing assistance in using ideas and scenarios about the future to better anticipate change, and design policies for dealing with that change. The Smart Data project aims to help meet policy needs with innovative data, and technical, organisational, legal and human capabilities, working closely with OECD Member countries and the broader data ecosystem.

New Approaches to Economic Challenges (NAEC)

The NAEC came into being, formally, in 2012, when the Meeting of the OECD Council at Ministerial Level (MCM) strongly endorsed it as a project on the basis of the 'New Approaches to Economic Challenges, Mandate, Governance and Next Steps' paper that urged the need for the project. However, its roots go back at least to the OECD's 1969 report on 'Problems of Modern Societies', the 1977 McCracken Report 'Towards Full Employment and Price Stability' and 'Social Cohesion and the Globalising Economy, (1997). In particular, its immediate roots can be found in the rethinking of economic and social policy sparked off by the impact of the Global Financial Crisis (GFC) in 2008–2009, and continued for several years as the impact of the GFC continued to be felt.

Much of the initial rethinking was summarised in 2009 in the 'OECD Strategic Response to the Financial and Economic Crisis', which focused on shorter-term responses to the crisis and two priority areas. The first was on policies regarding finance, competition and governance, with a pledge to work on strengthening and implementing principles and guidelines in these traditional focuses of OECD work. The second priority, the restoration of long-term growth, again, was an unsurprising emphasis, but it was argued that growth should be accompanied by an emphasis on 'low-carbon paths to growth, on eco-innovation, and on knowledge creation, all within a more equitable society that spreads opportunity and extends protection to the most vulnerable'. While these latter topics had been investigated at the OECD in the past, they had now come to the forefront of its work, a place they still occupy.

https://doi.org/10.1515/9783110735833-011

However, in this early period after the GFC, rethinking was somewhat compartmentalised, lacking a coherent strategy to pull it together and form the basis for applicable policy options. In retrospect, this is not surprising, for it took some years before a comprehensive understanding of what caused the GFC was achieved and, without that, the rethinking of policy proposals was, if not incoherent, then lacking in focus. The NAEC was an attempt to remedy this situation, to provide, first a comprehensive analysis of the causes of the GFC and the lessons that could be learnt from it, building on work already underway in many committees and Directorates, including work on where past OECD policy recommendations were ill-directed, and those that were more successful. NAEC's second aim was to draw on the results of its understanding of the causes of the GFC and the past impact of policies in order to identify key elements of a renewed framework to address complex and interrelated economic issues, a challenging aim. An initial objective was to develop what was described as a 'Strategic OECD Policy Agenda for Inclusive Growth', covering macroeconomic, structural and financial issues, and incorporating employment, social and environmental dimensions. However, this was soon spun off as a separate, horizontal project focused on reducing inequalities and promoting well-being, and is discussed in Chapter 8.

The NAEC project is led by the NAEC Group, chaired by the Secretary-General, with a wide range of Ambassadors, Committee Chairs and directors, in a multidisciplinary effort, and supported by a small Unit. It has a modest budget, based largely on voluntary contributions from the private sector, foundations and OECD Members. It is based, not in a Directorate or Centre with their established policy networks, but in the Office of the Secretary-General, giving it a degree of independence in its work – though this also makes it a target for sometimes critical attention and efforts to fold it into a Directorate.

NAEC's work, as indicated in its 2020 paper 'The New Approaches to Economic Challenges (NAEC) Initiative: Rejuvenating the Debate', has fallen into three broad, interlinked phases.

The First Phase, 2012–2016

In this first phase 29 linked projects were undertaken, focused on the causes of the crisis, the limitations of traditional economic modelling and approaches in understanding the crisis, and the need for new modelling and approaches to gain a better understanding. Many of its findings and recommendations were contained in its 2015 'Final NAEC Synthesis: New Approaches to Economic Challenges'. In brief, the report argued for a change in OECD perspectives and objectives, including:
- A greater focus on well-being and its distribution to ensure that growth delivers progress for all.
- Better integration of the financial sector and related risks in analyses.

- Analysing the global economy as a complex adaptive system, incorporating un-certainty, spill-overs, systemic risks and network effects.
- The adoption of a longer-term perspective that considers how economies are embedded in institutions shaped by history, social norms and political choices, enabling policies better tailored to countries' situations.
- Further developing and using strategic foresight to build plausible scenarios that assist in designing better policy options.
- The measurement of both stocks and flows of wealth, and natural, and social capital.
- The collection and analysis of a greater range of micro-data to identify the heterogeneity of households and firms, and facilitate analyses of inequality.
- The review, diversification and improvement of OECD modelling approaches, as well as a fuller understanding of their limitations.

These represented a wide and ambitious reform agenda, aimed at improving economic and social policy, an agenda that has been largely implemented in the years since the results of phase one were submitted to, and endorsed by, the MCM in 2015.

The Second Phase, 2016–2020

The second phase represented a marked change in direction for NAEC, examining the future of the economy, new directions in economic thought, and the policy implications of these developments, with a particular focus on the need for systems thinking, anticipation and resilience. It developed a wide range of external involvement in, and support for, its work. Cooperation on resilience, for example, with the International Institute for Applied Systems Analysis (IIASA) and the US Army Corps of Engineers, focused on averting system instability and collapse by developing greater system resilience – work that soon found an application in the case of the COVID-19 pandemic. NAEC has also become a focus for inter-disciplinary and often critical work on the economy.

Among the second phase's publications was the 2020 'Beyond Growth', which contributed to the debate initiated by Secretary-General Gurría's 2015 '21 for 21' proposal to consolidate and further transform the OECD by, in part, 'redefining the growth narrative to put the well-being of people at the centre of our efforts'. The paper was developed by an Advisory Group on a New Growth Narrative, set up by the Secretary-General in 2018, and brought together much of the earlier NAEC work in a more coherent narrative, proposing a new set of goals and measures of economic and social progress, as well as new frameworks and approaches to policy.

In an almost prescient fashion, the second phase resulted in NAEC's 2019 conference on 'Averting Systemic Collapse', which showed how growing complexity and interdependence, combined with aspirations for maximum efficiency and optimisation, plus the neglect of systemic resilience, had made economic and public health systems more susceptible to failure. It was a theme further elaborated in 'A Systemic Resilience Approach to Dealing with COVID-19 and Future Shocks', published shortly after the outbreak in April 2020.

The Third Phase, 2020 Onwards

At the time of writing, the third phase of NAEC's work was underway, focusing, again, on promoting new economic narratives and paradigms, building systemic resilience and developing new analytical tools and techniques and crisis simulation. It involves the NAEC Group on Confronting Planetary Emergencies and will concentrate on moving from analysis and diagnoses of systemic challenges to policy answers, including a new programme, 'A Systemic Recovery'. This work is marked by a serious concern for the resilience of the systems that hold societies together, as highlighted by the COVID-19 pandemic.

NAEC was born in the aftermath of the GFC and its third phase has begun in the midst of the COVID-19 crisis. The former provided an opportunity for NAEC to commence its work and the latter for NAEC to continue its work, focused on improving system capacities, resilience and developing new answers to policy challenges. Much of its work in phases two and three has criticised the limitations of orthodox economic thought and related approaches, with their overwhelming focus on efficiency, to the neglect of system capacity and resilience. This has been courageous in that much of the work of the OECD rests on such orthodoxy, and organisations are not generally keen to see their weaknesses revealed. It is to the credit of the OECD that it established NAEC, that it continues to fund its efforts, and that it listens to its analyses and recommendations – even when it does not always accept them.

The Strategic Foresight Unit (SFU)

Strategic foresight as defined by the OECD's SFU, is a structured and systematic way of using ideas about the future to anticipate and better prepare for change. It is about exploring different plausible futures that could arise, and the opportunities and challenges they could present, using those ideas to make better decisions in the present. It is not forecasting, with its emphasis on the search for an accurate picture of the future based on evidence and probability. In this broad sense, foresight has been a part of the OECD's work and methodological approaches since its establishment, even if, in earlier years, the term foresight was rarely used. In the last two decades the use of strategic foresight has become more frequent and explicit at the OECD, with, for example, a series of Technology Foresight Forums having been organised since 2005 in the Directorate for Science, Technology and Innovation.

Most famous of the OECD's earlier use of foresight was the 1976–1979 INTERFU-TURES Project, promoted by the Japanese government. Its aim was ambitious, to provide an assessment of 'alternative patterns of longer-term world economic development', so as to clarify the implications of these patterns for the strategic policy options open to Members. At its peak, it had a team of 15 full-time staff supported by a number of consultants.

In terms of its impact, 20 years after its completion, Wolfgang Michalski, Deputy Director of the Project and, from 1980 to 2001 Director of the Advisory Unit to OECD Secretary-Generals that later provided foresight advice, noted that from the start it generated suspicions in Member governments and that its largely scenario-based analysis touched upon many areas of great political or ideological sensitivity generating 'some discomfort', amongst governments and within some parts of the OECD Secretariat. In summary, it was too broad in scope and had little immediate impact on Members. It did, however, provide some important lessons, notably that longer-term work on economic and social issues at the OECD should be narrower in scope and focused on the needs of clearly defined constituencies and Members.

Nearly a quarter of a century later, in 1990, the OECD established the International Futures Programme (IFP), with a small number of staff, operating within the OECD's Advisory Unit to the Secretary-General, to whom it reported, and advised by an informal group of Ambassadors to the OECD. In its original form it persisted for 23 years, often organised around a major, thematically focused topic, with ministers and CEOs participating from early in each project.

The IFP had two related sets of activities, the first being the Forum for the Future, a platform for informal, high-level meetings among senior policy makers from government, business, research and civil society. Its aim was to test new ideas, develop fresh perspectives and advance the understanding of major economic and social issues. The second was a set of individual, OECD Futures projects undertaking multidisciplinary research and policy analyses on future-oriented themes, often as spin-offs from Forum for the Future Conferences.

The projects involved both governments and the private sector, and were a useful means for getting issues onto the OECD agenda, especially where there was no appropriate OECD Committee or Directorate to address the specific theme of a project. It was funded, initially, from the Part I budget, but increasingly successfully by voluntary contributions from a number of sources, as support for the IFP slowly fell among Members, as the 2005 Medium Term Orientations indicated. Among its many works and in the context of the GFC and COVID-19, one of its projects stands out, the Project on Emerging Systemic Risks (2002–2004), which presented a set of recommendations for better managing systemic risks in its 2004 publication 'Large Scale Disasters: Lessons Learned', and was followed by increasing OECD work on risk management policies.

In 2008–2009 the IFP began situating itself within the small, but rapidly expanding, international foresight community, and created, in collaboration with what was then UK Foresight, the OECD Government Foresight Network in order to foster exchanges among government foresight groups on strategic foresight. By 2011 there were 20 participating governments (OECD and non-OECD) and it had held a total of four meetings – in the UK, Canada, and at OECD, with Secretary-General Gurría attending the meeting at the OECD.

In 2011 the Director of the Secretary-General's Advisory Group, Michael Oborne, retired and the Secretary-General used the opportunity to restructure by moving the IFP team into the Directorate for Science, Technology and Innovation (DSTI), although the team advised the Secretary-General that a continuing foresight unit in his Office would be valuable. The IFP team was then based within DSTI as a specialised group (later being renamed as Innovation Policies for Space and Oceans, IPSO), focussing on innovation policies for the space economy and the ocean economy, streams of work created and initially developed by the IFP.

In 2013 a new Strategic Foresight Unit was established in the OSG, initially with only one member, with a rather different role to its predecessor, focused on embedding strategic foresight work into the Organisation's activities, rather than creating and developing projects. The NAEC unit had emphasised the lack of foresight and innovation scanning work at the OECD in its analysis of the causes of the GFC, and recommended the adoption of a longer-term perspective, well-informed by scenario development and horizon scanning, by further developing strategic foresight. The need for a continuing foresight capacity had also been urged by members of the IFP before its transfer. NAEC's recommendation was endorsed by Secretary-General Gurría and approved by the MCM, and the outcome was the creation of the SFU, led by Dr Angela Wilkinson.

The SFU was given three initial objectives:

-   To pilot the use of strategic foresight for supporting high level policy dialogue, as achieved, for example, in the scenario-based policy discussion at the 2015 Ministerial Council and the discussion of megatrends during the Global Strategy Group meeting in December 2015.
-   To create a new coordinated horizon-scanning system for use throughout the OECD, feeding, for example, into the OECD's megatrends analysis and the Next Production Revolution initiative.
-   To build upon the Government Foresight Network, established by the IFP in 2009.

While good progress was made in regard to these objectives, the SFU was hampered by its very limited staffing capacity, especially in its important efforts to integrate foresight across Directorates. As a result, much of its work did not take place in or with Directorates and was dependent on the expertise of a very limited number of individuals. In 2016 an upgrading of its capacity was undertaken, including the recruitment of Duncan Cass-Beggs as the Counsellor for Strategic Foresight. The aim was to bring a stronger future focus to global dialogue on major policy issues by working more closely, not only with OECD staff, but with Member governments to help ensure that emerging changes and critical uncertainties are appropriately considered in OECD policy analysis and advice. It included the provision of foresight workshops for Directorates and coordinating a committee of 'foresight focal points' drawn from Directorates.

While not initiating major policy projects, the SFU has provided a range of scenarios in support of projects, such as scenarios for digital transformation in support of the Going Digital programme in 2017–2018. It also provided major support for the 'Towards 2035 Making Migration and Integration Policies Future Ready', paper for the 2020 OECD Ministerial Meeting of Migration and Integration, working with a Task Force of eight Member countries in three foresight workshops to develop eight scenarios, later discussed by the Working Party on Migration. It also helped provide, as part of the 'Preventing Ageing Unequally', project, a policy foresight model to assess the impact and linkages of health, employment and retirement patterns on inequality among older age groups. Importantly, it has also contributed to the OECD's efforts in relation to COVID-19.

The SFU now increasingly works with Member countries to support their foresight efforts, including working with Iceland's Futures Committee to upgrade strategic foresight capacities and similar projects with Slovenia, Slovakia, Estonia and Latvia, complementing the OECD's 'Going National' endeavours. In 2020, for example, at the now annual Government Foresight Meeting, hosted by the OECD, it worked with the European Environment Agency to investigate 'wild cards', or low probability, high impact events in its environmental work.

Smart Data

The Smart Data strategy is based on the recognition that the development of sound policies on digitalisation, globalisation, sustainability, well-being, and so on requires a solid evidence base. It was believed that to develop such evidence there was a need to access more data sources, continue to modernise existing data processes, and leverage advanced data science techniques, while ensuring the core value of the OECD in providing trusted, high quality evidence continued. More granular and timely data were considered necessary to complement existing statistics. This would enable micro-level analysis, and improve forecasts and 'nowcasts', while combining different sources would enable 'multidimensional insight and modelling'.

Meeting this policy demand with data innovation required considerable and continuous investment in 'data commons'. The Smart Data strategy is pursuing the development of technical, organisational, legal, and human capabilities, in close collaboration with Member countries and the broader 'data ecosystem'. The strategy has two broad goals in mind: Integrating the Data Cycle; and Embracing Smart Data.

The first of these requires modernising the collection, analysis, processing, and dissemination of data, mainly from established sources, such as statistical or policy reporting by national governments. This aims at increasing the efficiency in data operations, by overcoming fragmentation in tools, processes and data models, and enforcing a 'quality by design' approach. The cornerstone is the harmonisation of data models, enabling data integration, efficiency and accessibility.

Embracing Smart Data involves accessing alternative data sources and using data science techniques such as machine learning or text mining, to supplement existing evidence ('nowcasting') by facilitating more granularity (either spatially, or on criteria such as gender or income distribution) and higher frequency, as well as bringing about new correlations and predictors that enable deeper analysis or improved simulation of policy effects and forecasts. The Smart Data Strategy pursues these goals through six interconnected data commons where innovation and investment are expected to take place: data governance; sourcing; platform; quality framework; skills; and engagement.

Smart Data also seeks to cultivate and connect open ecosystems for data innovation, connecting experts from other international organisations (such as the ILO and UNECEF) and Member countries, as well as academia, start-ups, NGOs, and large digital players. It facilitates sharing and co-constructing intangible assets (open source, open data, open algorithms and open knowledge) as public goods, in order to support 'Better policies for Better lives'. The development of data commons with organisations sharing common goals is undertaken through the Statistical Information System Collaboration Community (SIS-CC), a reference open-source community for official statistics.

The strategy has received substantial funding through voluntary contributions and is managed through good cooperation with other Directorates by about 25 staff in a Division of the Statistics and Data Directorate, dealing with the challenge of integrating its operation horizontally across all Directorates. The strategy has already achieved important results – establishing data governance based on communities of practice; establishing a data sourcing practice with commercial data providers as well as a non-profit data-sharing framework; renewing capabilities in the area of data processing and data dissemination; and renewing the OECD the data quality framework, introducing a number of technology-enabled innovations. But multiple, sometimes tough, challenges remain to be addressed in the coming years, such as: systematic upskilling of staff in the area of data science techniques; gaining much wider access to confidential micro-data from public and private organisations; and establishing systematic data and algorithmic reproducibility of the evidence and models used by OECD to inform policy analysis. From that perspective, the smart data strategy should be seen as a long-term challenge and multi-year investment effort, relying on a 'business model' that should more and more involve the 'ecosystem'.

Conclusion

NAEC, the SFU and the Smart Data strategy are at the cutting edge of OECD change and development, exploring and testing new and modified systems, scenarios and methods that help keep the Organisation near the forefront of policy research, analysis and recommendations. As a result, their work is sometimes viewed with varying degrees of caution, but always with interest as to its applicability in the work of the Directorates. Each of the three has the potential to bring about significant change at the OECD, as is the case for NAEC's work on resilience, a concept and an approach that has been rapidly assimilated into the organisation's policy research, analysis and policy recommendations, spurred on by the impacts of the GFC and COVID-19.

12 From Radiation Health to COVID-19: Health Work at the OECD

Health work at the OECD developed rapidly in the twenty-first century from modest beginnings. It has focused heavily on the comparative performance of health systems, and the collection of standardised data from OECD Members that enables more detailed analysis and, in turn, more specific policy development and recommendations. A stimulus for the work has been the growing share of Members' economies accounted for by health systems, faced with ageing populations and the increased incidence of dementia and Alzheimer's, as well as technological change and low productivity in the sector. More broadly, the need to make health systems more efficient and people centred has stimulated work on how to measure what health systems deliver to people; the health and economic impact of tackling obesity and alcohol; the dynamics of health innovation (e.g., new drugs, medical techniques); and ways to improve the use of health data while respecting patient privacy. Most recently, it now addresses the challenge of COVID-19. This chapter summarises the origins of OECD health work, its rapid development in scale and scope after 2000, and the impact of COVID-19 on that work.

Origins and Development of Health Work

Heath policy had been of interest to the members of the OECD's forerunner, the Organisation for European Economic Co-operation (OEEC) in the 1950s, but always as a secondary issue, for example, work on health protection for persons exposed to ionizing radiation, undertaken by the European Nuclear Energy Agency (ENEA). Health work gradually gained a greater priority from the late 1970s and 1980s onwards. Nevertheless, other than the important collation, analysis and reporting of health expenditure data provided by Members from 1985, and funded by a voluntary contribution from the USA, the OECD did not initiate substantive and ongoing work on health policy until the 1990s, with, for example, the 1990 OECD report on 'Health Care Systems in Transition: the Search for Efficiency'. This work was inspired largely by rapidly rising health expenditures in Member countries and their search for policy solutions.

The 1990 report led to a 1994 meeting of 12 OECD Health Ministers, officials and academics to discuss health reforms. They called for more OECD work in this area, therefore stimulating work on health policy, focusing on the development of composite health indicators and measures that would enable more effective policy. Perhaps the most important development was in 1996, following an Ad Hoc Meeting of Experts in Health Statistics, calling for the development of international standards for data on healthcare expenditure and financing, leading to the now well-known

https://doi.org/10.1515/9783110735833-012

OECD System of Health Accounts, first released in 2000. Health was also increasingly prominent in the influential annual OECD Economic Surveys, accompanied by the evaluation of health reforms in the Directorate of Employment, Labour and Social Affairs (DELSA), and the examination of market-related reforms in the health sector by Public Management (PUMA, later renamed as Public Governance).

The 1998 OECD Ministerial Council Meeting stressed the increasing health challenges faced by OECD Members and urged the need for further work on health. Two years of discussions on what should be done came to a positive conclusion when a new, three-year, horizontal (i.e., cross-Directorate) Health Project was approved in 2001. In part, the Project was the result of an earlier, critical reaction from several OECD Members, including the USA and Australia, to the surprisingly low rankings they had received in the 2000 WHO World Health Report, and the methodological weaknesses they found in that Report. Members' dissatisfaction sharpened their support for the Health Project. The Project was funded, for the most part, by a contribution from the Secretary-General's Central Priorities Fund and by voluntary contributions from Members.

The Project focused on the measurement and analysis of health systems in OECD countries and the factors that affected performance, including the measurement of income-related equity of access to health care; nurse shortages; waiting times; private health insurance; new, health-related technologies; and long-term care for the fragile elderly. On the basis of the findings, a framework for describing and assessing health systems in OECD countries was developed, as well as policy recommendations.

The Health Project also provided impetus for further work on value for money from health spending; the development of indicators regarding the technical quality of medical care; approaches to monitoring and improving health care; as well as the development of a new work stream on the economics of public health and non-communicable diseases.

A report reviewing the Health Project was well received by Council in 2004, and the remainder of the 2000s saw health work developing further, with a high level of support from most Members and the then new Secretary-General, Angel Gurría. A further recognition of the new prominence accorded to health was the establishment in 2007 of a standing Health Committee and an increase in health funding.

Health Work, 2011–2021

The extent, reputation and importance of the OECD's work on health expanded rapidly from 2006 to 2021, reflected in the wide range of publications that have resulted, especially on assessing and improving the quality and performance of Members' national health systems. The work is important because average health spending as a share of GDP across the OECD was around 8.8% on average even before the COVID-19 pandemic, and health systems are faced with a range of major challenges which the pandemic has dramatically illustrated.

The influence of OECD health work also grew rapidly in this period, including, in more recent years, in relation to the G20's Health Working Group, established under the German Presidency in 2017. The aim of the G20 Group was to develop a shared international agenda on issues such as strengthening health-care systems, reducing malnutrition, health-crisis management, and scaling up the fight against pandemics. The OECD was requested to coordinate and prepare, together with the WHO, FAO and OIE, a report on tackling antimicrobial resistance and, in 2019, to prepare a background report on healthy ageing for the Japanese presidency of the G20. The OECD also provided support to work on health under the G7, for example in the context of the Summit on Dementia in 2014, work on universal health coverage in 2016. and work on primary health care in 2019.

Much of the work on health under the supervision of the Health Committee in 2011 was focussed on improving the ability to measure health system performance (including the use of information on quality of health care), and promoting value for money for the system as a whole as well as in different health sectors (hospital, primary care, long-term care, pharmaceutical) and for specific diseases. The work had met with, and continued to receive, strong support from most OECD Members, as indicated, for example, by the priority 1 ranking it received in the OECD's 2012 Medium Term Orientations Process (MTO). The largest proportion of health funding was to the continuing and expanding data work of the Health Division and the Health Committee, developing internationally-comparable information and indicators of health, health systems and health expenditures, often described as the building blocks of much of the work of the Committee, funded from Part I of the Budget. A high priority was also given to work on health care quality, value for money and the economics of prevention, notably as regards obesity and alcohol, the latter two exciting the attention of related industry groups.

Health work was guided by the conclusions from the 2010 Health Ministers' meeting that encouraged a continuing emphasis on monitoring health performance and health accounts work, especially the Health Care Quality Indicators project, requesting the Health Committee to do further work on identifying good practice and how to improve it. It also asked for work on:

- The development of health skills and the implications of the growing demand for health professionals, the challenges this posed and possible policy solutions.
- The links between health, economic growth and well-being.
- Medical practice variations, with a focus on in-country variations and the analysis of possible causes for variations, followed by the examination of policy options to reduce unwanted variations that used scare resources, to be completed in 2013.
- The economics of prevention, focusing on alcohol abuse, with its damaging impacts on the individual, labour markets and society at large, led by an expert

group, established in 2010. The project examined trends and disparities in consumption and outcomes and the impact of alcohol policies.

The trend of projects involving a number of Committees and Directorates, that commenced with the Health Project, continued with a major project on mental health and its work implications with the Employment, Labour and Social Affairs Committee (ELSAC) and the Health Committee. This work focused on ways of integrating health, employment and social services, and on a range of country studies, completed in 2014. Similarly, work with the Economics Department began in 2010 on a study of existing institutional models of health systems and efficiency. Early work on the financial sustainability of health systems also led to the establishment of a joint network by the Health Committee and the Working Party of Senior Budget Officials (SBO) in the Directorate for Public Governance, as a forum for analysis and sharing useful practices on improving health system financial sustainability.

Work with non-member countries also increased, in line with the new OECD Global Relations Strategy (GRS) and the requirement that all substantive Committees – including health – develop their own global relations strategies and action plans, within the context of the GRS. This led to further links with OECD accession candidates and the BRICS, building on established links with the WHO and other international organisations.

Efforts to engage with non-members also takes place in the context of co-operation with the WHO Regional Offices. For example, a Health Care Quality Improvement Network was set up in Asia-Pacific with WHO Western Pacific Regional and South East Asia regional offices. Co-operation with international organisations also includes Eurostat. For example, the OECD, Eurostat and WHO developed a joint arrangement for health data collection in Europe. Further work also continued on a framework to improve the comparability and availability of data on private health expenditure.

The relationship with the EU is particularly close. For example, the European Commission has supported work on the development of the European Edition of Health at a Glance and, more recently, the State of Health in the EU; indicators of patient safety; analysis on public health including alcohol abuse, obesity, and antimicrobial resistance; work on the health workforce; and the recent flagship initiative on Patient-Reported Indicators Surveys.

The work on ageing, combined with an increased international focus and collaboration on dementia, led to the OECD being more heavily involved in this work, which had commenced in 2004. The OECD participated in the G8 Dementia Summit of December 2013, which led to the establishment of the World Dementia Council. It also strongly supported the first Ministerial Conference on Global Action Against Dementia in 2015, organised by the WHO. A number of dementia-related projects resulted, including the Working Party on Biotechnology, Nanotechnology and Converging Technology's healthy ageing and biomedical innovation for dementia and Alzheimer's disease research (2015). However, progress in dealing with dementia remains slow. Too many countries lack the data infrastructure to be able to monitor quality of care for people living with dementia, for example, as shown in the OECD's 2018 report 'Care Needed: Improving the Lives of People with Dementia'.

A Hospital Performance Project initiated in 2015 was completed in 2017. The scope and scale of the data collected was path-breaking as it was the first time that hospital-level performance data had been collated and compared across OECD countries in America, Europe and Asia. The results were published in 'Health at a Glance 2019', Chapter 6, and have since been extended, for example, to focus on stroke mortality.

The continuing interest in, and support for, the OECD's work on health by Secretary-General Gurría was further illustrated in 2016, when he was appointed as a co-chair of the UN's High-Level Commission on Health, Employment and Economic Growth, along with the heads of the WHO and the ILO, and chaired by the French and South African Presidents. The Commission's work was supported by the OECD, working together with the WHO and the ILO.

Most of the health data collected by the OECD up to 2015 have focused largely on inputs, activities and costs, with relatively few measures of outcomes, notably those directly reported by patients. As a result, policymakers have only a limited view of how well their health systems respond to patients' needs. In 2015, as part of an effort to remedy this neglect, a High-Level Reflection Group was set up to discuss options to improve the collection and reporting of healthcare outcomes across OECD populations. It recommended that the OECD extend and deepen the benchmarking of health system performance by collecting patient-reported indicators, with a focus on enabling international comparisons.

The recommendation met with a positive response from OECD Health Ministers at their 2017 meeting, where they requested the OECD to help them reorient their health systems to become more 'people-centred', a move that necessitated the development of new performance data and led to the Patient Reported Indicator Surveys (PaRIS) project to assist governments in understanding how their health systems could better meet people's needs. The PaRIS surveys focus on people living with chronic conditions and will be the first international survey of patient-reported health outcomes and experiences of adults living with chronic conditions. The surveys are being developed in a three-phase process, to be completed in 2023, assisted by a Patient Advisory Panel.

The increasing extent of health-related data gathered by the OECD soon drew the attention of officials to the issue of health data governance, mindful of the efforts of OECD Members to improve their data governance frameworks and the variability across countries in the take up of internationally agreed standards for data elements within electronic health records. The OECD also found that certain key data elements lacked agreed international standards. The lack of agreed standards creates an obstacle to multi-country studies and to internationally comparable health and health care indicators, as found by the OECD's 2013 publication 'Strengthening Health Information Infrastructure for Health Care Quality Governance: Good Practices, New Opportunities and Data Privacy Protection Challenges'. In particular, the issue of threats to privacy came to the fore and a two-year study was undertaken by the OECD's Health Care Quality Indicators Expert Group in 2013–2014, assisted by the OECD's Working Party on Security and Privacy in a Digital Economy, that had been examining data governance and privacy in a broader context. The result was the 2015 OECD 'Health Data Governance' Report, that stressed the need for periodical, international reviews to maximise societal benefits and minimise societal risks as new data sources and new technologies were introduced.

The Report and further studies led to a joint proposal to Council from the Health Committee and the Committee on Digital Economy Policy for an OECD Recommendation on Health Data Governance. The Committees stressed that several OECD Members lacked a coordinated public policy framework to guide health data use and sharing practices to protect privacy, enable efficiencies, promote quality and foster innovative research. The proposal stressed the need to support greater harmonisation among members' health data governance frameworks, so that more countries could participate in multi-country statistical and research projects, while protecting privacy and data security. Council adopted the proposal in December 2016 and instructed the Health Committee to monitor implementation of the Recommendation and report back within five years. A 2019 survey that monitored the implementation of the Recommendation showed variability across countries in its adoption and proposed a further monitoring plan. A Health Committee report is to be prepared for submission to the OECD Council in late 2021/early 2022.

OECD Response to COVID-19

The outbreak of the global COVID-19 pandemic in January 2020 made the year an unforgettable one. A new virus with no vaccine and with little known about appropriate pharmaceuticals or other treatments to be used caused widespread concern, if not panic. Epidemiological modelling, accepted as forecasts, projected many thousands of deaths and led to the introduction of non-pharmaceutical interventions (NPIs) such as restricting travel and shutting down societies and economies, despite a World Health Organisation report on influenza-like pandemics the previous October recommending against such NPIs – at least in part because of their social and economic costs. To support government efforts in this unprecedented crisis, the OECD provided new data and analysis on containment and mitigation policies; the role of testing, tracking and tracing; how to build health system resilience; vaccines; and the impact of the pandemic on mental health.

The pandemic presented a considerable challenge to the OECD – a challenge to which the Organisation rose quite well. It not only used its analytical and communications capacities to assist in the global response to the pandemic, but seized the opportunity it created to invigorate its 'Green Growth' and 'Inclusive Growth' agendas, essentially following the advice to 'never allow a good crisis to go to waste when it's an opportunity to do things that you had never considered, or that you didn't think were possible'. Whereas the global recession following the responses to the pandemic might have threatened to displace the OECD's social and environmental agendas, the Organisation emphasised the need to 'Build Back Better,' – or 'Build Forward Better' as often stated by Gurría – appropriating a slogan previously applied to recovery efforts after natural disasters such as earthquakes.

A key feature of the OECD is the value it provides by creating networks among experts – its own staff and those of governments and beyond. Even with travel made difficult, the OECD employed its Forum Network to bring together the thoughts of both OECD experts and others from around the world and all parts of society to provide commentary on the COVID-19 pandemic, both discussing solutions and raising critical points on topics such as the civil liberties aspects of responses. Such opinions did not necessarily represent the views of the OECD. Contributions on COVID-19 on The Forum Network began with a post entitled 'Tax in the time of COVID-19' from Pascal Saint-Amans, Director of the Centre for Tax Policy and Administration, and 'How can teachers and school systems respond to the COVID-19 pandemic? Some lessons from TALIS' by Andreas Schleicher, Director, Education and Skills. These were posted on 23 March 2020, quite early in the pandemic. At the time of writing, there have been in excess of 350 contributions (including some in multiple languages). There were also blog posts on health system resilience and vaccines.

More formally, the OECD leveraged its policy expertise and launched new initiatives to help countries, both Members and non-members, respond to the pandemic with informed analyses and guidance on best practices. It did so by launching a Digital Hub on Tackling the Coronavirus, providing a single entry point to the OECD's analysis on the economic and social impacts of COVID-19.

The Hub provided a 'one-stop shop' on all things COVID-19, including a data gallery with original data visualisations related to the pandemic and its implications, allowing users to filter according to global economy, resilient healthcare, social challenges and the green recovery. It also permitted users to search for topics by key words, to examine data over time and by country or region. These four topics, together with inclusive recovery, could be explored further on the Hub. The data could also be shared on social media. At the time of writing, the Hub had received over 2.8 million unique visitors.

The Hub also included a series allowing key policy responses to be examined, bringing together data, analyses and recommendations on various topics to help address what was recognised as an emerging health, economic and societal crisis. The responses focused on the vulnerable sectors of society and the economy, providing guidance on short-term measures needed in affected sectors, as well as analysis on longer-term consequences and impacts of COVID-19, with a view to recovery with co-ordinated policy responses. Also included is a Country Policy Tracker, which allows a country-by-country search to explore what individual countries are doing to limit the spread of the virus, and assist people, small businesses and the economy.

Underlying fiscal and economic data, as well as that on health and employment and social issues, can also be downloaded.

In 2020, three Ministerial Council Roundtables were held: one on the economic outlook; one on employment and social protection; and a third on the environment. The Roundtables fed into the work of the 2020 Ministerial Council Meeting held on 28–29 October on the theme of 'The Path to Recovery: Strong, Resilient, Green and Inclusive'.

The OECD also supported the G20 and other international fora in developing a collective response to the pandemic and its impact, and made use of the theme of resilience and a range of innovative economic tools and methods developed by the New Approaches to Economic Challenges (NAEC) Initiative that had been launched in 2012.

The OECD also organised a number of workshops with Member countries to share insights and discuss policy options for both dealing with the pandemic and assisting with economic recovery. The horizontal nature of the response to COVID-19 gave rise to similar themes to various other activities. For example, in May 2020 the Global Anti-Corruption and Integrity Forum held a Webinar series on 'Anti-corruption and integrity: safeguards for a resilient COVID-19 response and recovery', and the Global Forum on Responsible Business Conduct a virtual event on 'COVID-19 and Responsible Business Conduct'. It also prepared a series of policy briefs with the same aims as the workshops. There was also work on regional responses to COVID-19 and the OECD analysed responses to the crisis in South East European economies, MENA countries, Central Asia, Latin America and the Caribbean, ASEAN member states and Africa.

Building Back Better – Building Forward Better

The focus on economic recovery after the COVID-19 crisis might have deflected attention away from Green Growth, Inclusive Growth, and NAEC initiatives, but the crisis was harnessed in support of these by insisting that the recovery should involve 'Building Back Better' by incorporating these emphases.

Building Back Better was a slogan initially used in relation to recovery from natural disasters, first after the 2004 Indian Ocean Tsunami, and then adopted by the United Nations Office for Disaster Risk Reduction in the Sendai Framework for Disaster Risk Reduction. Secretary-General Gurría himself had used it in that context in remarks at a Development Assistance Committee (DAC) Senior Level Meeting and International Panel Discussion in April 2010 with the title 'Haiti: Are We on Course to Build Back Better?' While Prince Charles and the World Economic Forum had enunciated a similar desire to harness the sense of crisis to a 'Great Reset' of global capitalism in May 2020, the first use of the slogan in relation to COVID-19 was by the World Resources Institute on 12 March and then the We Mean Business Coalition on 3 April, both very quick to use the pandemic as a driver for climate change policy.

The OECD was the first international organisation to harness the slogan to create support for social and environmental action, with the publication on 5 June 2020 of *Building Back Better: A Sustainable, Resilient Recovery after COVID-19.*, one of 182 OECD Policy Responses to COVID-19 at the time of writing.

Impact of the Pandemic on the OECD

While the coronavirus pandemic provided the OECD with the opportunity to empower its pre-existing agendas, it also presented challenges to 'business as usual' for the Organisation. The participation of policymakers from the global membership in the numerous Committees and working parties is, ordinarily, an important part of its operations. The interactions among the representatives of Member governments, as well as with relevant members of the Secretariat, form the basis for significant global policy networks that are functional not just for the OECD, but also for other global policy arenas.

The pandemic saw varying kinds of restrictions on travel, with many national borders closed or open only after quarantine had been observed. The conduct of OECD business was able to continue, thanks to the widespread use of virtual meetings and the use of webinars, as well as the other electronic media. Doubtless, these media will continue to be used in the future, but perhaps run the risk of weakening these global networks if not reinforced periodically by face-to-face interaction.

The economic impact of the pandemic also created problems for some of the core functions of the Organisation, such as its policy recommendations and economic forecasting. The 2008 financial crisis had given it recent experience of dealing with crises, but the pandemic response still contained some unprecedented elements. For example, at the end of May 2020 the Organisation produced a working paper 'What Policies for Greening the Crisis Response and Economic Recovery? Lessons Learned from Past Green Stimulus Measures and Implications for the COVID-19 Crisis' (Environment Working Paper No. 164). It was also able to maintain its biannual *Economic Outlook* reports with June and December issues, as well as a supplement in September which updated G20 country projections that had been made in the June issue.

Conclusion

OECD work on health, from limited beginnings, has become a central focus at the OECD, though increasingly impacted, as with most areas of the Organisation, by tight financial constraints. It has often been carried out in collaboration with other international organisations, notably the EU and the WHO, particularly data collection and analysis of national health expenditures. The future will see rapidly expanded work on the impact of, and recovery from, COVID-19, including a range of health issues, for example, mental health, the modelling of the pandemic, and measures to promote future health systems resilience.

13 Conclusion

In 2011, we published a book on the OECD that coincided with its 50th anniversary: *The OECD: A Study in Organisational Adaptation.* As that subtitle suggests, the Organisation had adapted to its changing environment since its formation in 1961. This book shows that this process has accelerated in the decade since 2011, as that environment has undergone even more rapid change, marked by the effects of two crises.

Scholars often write of organisations existing in 'punctuated equilibrium'; the Global Financial Crisis and the COVID-19 pandemic have certainly provided substantial punctuations to whatever equilibrium the OECD enjoyed in 2011. Yet, the Organisation has not only weathered those crises, but has flourished in them – thanks particularly to the dynamic, energetic and entrepreneurial leadership of its Secretary-General, Angel Gurría, who took up the role in 2006 and has steered the OECD to a significant place in the centre of global economic governance and as a 'do tank' (to use his expression) rather than a 'think tank', as it was previously often called.

Many of the strands of these changes began under his predecessor, Donald Johnston, but Johnston expressed frustration that the changes he saw as necessary were difficult to achieve in a 'member-owned' intergovernmental organisation, where the dominant decision rule of 'mutual agreement' meant that a single negative vote by a Member at Council meetings could frustrate any attempt at change. Changes were made, such as the reform of the budget system, led by the Australian Ambassador Ian Forsyth, who drove a belated adoption of programme budgeting in the Organisation that put itself forward as the exemplar of best practice financial management. Limited Qualified Majority Voting was also introduced for some purposes, but has proved of little use.

The relevance of the OECD was, however, being challenged. The rise of the 'Asian Tiger' economies and the end of Communism had led to it accounting for a diminished percentage of the global economy. Under Johnston, programmes of Enlargement and Enhanced Engagement were developed, the latter allowing co-operation with countries like Russia and China, but progress was slow. That was to change under Gurría's leadership.

There were also developments in the OECD's relationship to other international actors. In the case of the G7, and later the G20, this was because these groupings not possess any independent policy analytic capacity other than the agencies of their member governments. They were thus unable to produce and consider research that was seen to be untainted by national perspectives. That began to change, particularly with work on global tax policy with a reference in 1996 from the G7 requesting the OECD to work in that area.

Gurría, as Mexican Finance Minister at the time of the formation of the G20 at ministerial level, saw the potential in that grouping, and as early as 2004 advocated

https://doi.org/10.1515/9783110735833-013

for its elevation to the level of leaders of government. He did not explicitly push for a role for the OECD at that time, but, once appointed and prior to assuming office, he stated in an interview with the *New York Times* in late 2005 that he hoped the Organisation could play a greater role in supporting the G7. The Global Financial Crisis (GFC) that hit in 2008 provided both the need and the opportunity for the progression of this idea, especially as the G20 at leaders' level replaced the G7 as the effective forum for these issues.

The GFC required a response at a near global level and at a higher level than finance ministers. There was value in, if not 'minilateralism', then a restricted membership to improve the chances of reaching agreement. Heads of government were also able to make commitments that no finance minister could without consulting their capital. Gurría campaigned to insinuate the OECD into the G20 at leaders' level from its formation in 2008. However – perceived as the 'Club of the Rich' – close engagement was resisted, initially by China and several developing countries.

As we show in Chapter 10, the breakthrough came in April 2009 at the second G20 meeting in London, when the president of the meeting, United Kingdom Prime Minister Gordon Brown phoned Gurría in the presence of Barack Obama, Angel Merkel, Nicolas Sarkozy, and (significantly) Hu Jintao to invite the OECD to undertake further work on global tax policy, because the conduct of those avoiding national taxes was highlighted by the crisis. The Secretary-General then demonstrated considerable leadership in ensuring that the OECD was invited to attend subsequent meetings, and to appoint a Sherpa to participate in preparatory sessions before subsequent Summits.

Gurría's enthusiastic and energetic leadership also led to an enhanced global role for the Organisation, especially by recruiting Members, non-members and even private actors to provide voluntary contributions to support activities that could not be funded from the Part I Budget due to various constraints. This has led to some recent tensions between the Secretary-General and the Members represented on the Council, especially over the balance of influence.

The crisis resulting from the COVID-19 pandemic has also provided impetus for more reform, and Gurría has driven the process further, with the creation of the OECD Centre on Well-Being, Inclusiveness, Sustainability and Equal Opportunity (WISE), for example.

The result is that the OECD of today – with programmes on Inclusive Growth, Green Growth, Climate, Well-Being, Going Global, Going National, Going Digital, and so on – has evolved considerably from the OECD of 2011. While reforms were attempted prior to 2011, the Organisation has since become a much more dynamic, globally-oriented international organisation – perhaps less of an *intergovernmental* organisation – the value of which is more greatly recognised by its Members, and, more significantly, its non-members.

Moreover, as the chapters in this book illustrate, the last decade has also seen major developments in the OECD's methods, many of which were modified to improve the Organisation's monitoring and surveillance activities after the shock of the GFC. There has also been a marked growth in horizontal, multi-disciplinary, cross-Directorate work, some on a project basis, others on a more permanent format.

The changes that have been put in place are also reflected in an increase in the OECD's staff, up from 2880 in 2012 (of whom 2477 were officials), to 3859 in 2021 (of whom 3289 are officials), an increase of 32.6% for staff and 32.4% for officials. The single largest increase came in the broad area of global relations, largely in the Global Relations Secretariat, up from a mere handful in 2011 to over 200 in 2021 – mostly because of an increase in voluntary contributions and having taken several programmes from other areas. Membership also increased, up from 34 to 38. In addition, the budget increased by 15%, up from €342 million in 2011 to €393 million in 2020. Part I of the budget, that is financed by all Members, increased by 12.2%, while resources financed by special arrangements, notably voluntary contributions, have doubled over the period, to account for over 40% of the Part I resources in 2020.

There have been a limited number of major changes to the Directorates and Centres, which are responsible for the policy outputs of the OECD. The most obvious of these has been the growth in the number of Centres, up from three in 2011 (Centre for Educational Research and Innovation, Centre for Entrepreneurship, SMEs, and Local Development, and Centre for Tax Policy and Administration) to nine in 2021. The six new centres are the Centre on Well-being, Inclusion, Sustainability and Equal Opportunity, Centre for Skills, Global Blockchain Policy Centre, Centre on Philanthropy, Centre on Green Finance and Investment, and Centre for Opportunity and Equality, though some are small units within existing Directorates. Also, the Centre for Entrepreneurship, SMEs and Local Development was enlarged and renamed the Centre for Entrepreneurship, SMEs, Regions and Cities, and the Centre for Tax Policy and Administration increased in size as its work expanded.

The Directorates changed relatively little over the decade. The Directorate for Education gained a Centre for Skills; the Public Governance and Territorial Development Directorate lost Territorial Development to the Centre for Entrepreneurship, SMEs, Regions and Cities; the Directorates for Employment, Labour and Social Affairs and for Statistics lost functions to the new Centre on Well-being, Inclusion, Sustainability and Equal Opportunity (the latter is overseen by the Committee on Statistics and Statistical Policy and the Employment, Labour and Social Affairs Committee); and the Directorate for Science, Technology and Industry dropped Industry from its title, replacing it with Innovation, in line with its increased work on the topic.

There is no doubt that the OECD is very relevant to its Members and to global economic governance. This is reinforced by the results of the OECD's Programme Implementation Report for 2017–2018, based on the views of its Members, which rated 97% of its policy outputs as of High Quality and reported that all of those outputs were used by policymakers in national capitals. More significantly, 81% of those were rated as a 'Basis for Policy Change' by one or more Members, and 100% of Output Results were rated High Impact or above by one or more Members.

The immediate and future challenge for the OECD is to help its Members 'build back better' from COVID-19, a challenge the Organisation is very well-placed to meet, having gone through a period of vital, transformative change under the leadership of Secretary-General Gurría. He has provided his successor, Australian Mathias Cormann, with the strong, organisational base that he needs to achieve his 'Vision Statement for Secretary-General of the OECD' in the years ahead.